# Frances Kitchin

**DAVID & CHARLES**

Newton Abbot   London
North Pomfret (Vt)   Vancouver

# Contents

*(Approximate guide to oven temperatures 6)*

# Introduction

Both my grandmothers lived in the Langport area of Somerset. I loved my maternal grandmother dearly and the only disappointment she ever caused me was to die when I was in my early teens. I never knew my paternal grandmother as she lived from 1871 to 1939, but I do have her hand-written recipe book. She was a farmer's wife and like my aunt was very fond of cooking. Her recipes are included in this book together with those of her contemporaries who lived in the same area. Many of the recipes are taken from a hand-written book that I bought for 5p from a junk shop in Langport. It contains a collection of family recipes written by a mother for her daughter on the latter's marriage. It is obvious that this little recipe book was well used, the daughter adding her favourite recipes to those of her mother. These old hand-written books make interesting reading as they are not only devoted to cookery: in one of them there is a page headed 'The Harvest Supper List' under which are listed the items required for this annual event.

I have resisted the temptation to change the presentation of these recipes or 'receipts' as they were sometimes called and you will find the writers were not so particular about precise oven temperatures as today's cook is. The ranges the writers used were difficult to control, the temperature varying with each addition of fuel and depending upon the way the wind was blowing.

Granny's recipes on the whole were simple and the cost of the ingredients even today is low. Most of the ingredients my grandmother used were freely available on the farm and as a good Home Economist she made the best possible use of them.

Frances Kitchin
Witcombe, 1978

# For a rainy day:
## the larder and store-cupboard

In all large farmhouses you would find a large walk-in cupboard—the larder. Its floor was stone —usually flagstones—and there was a small window so that it was always cool. It could be rather damp as the flagstones used to sweat badly with the changing weather conditions. On the floor there would be a very large earthenware crock which housed the bread. When its earthenware lid broke, it was usually replaced by a wooden one. Another large crock would be used for storing eggs that were being pickled. The walls supported many shelves and more often than not there would be a salting tray. This was a huge tray made from lead with a lip at the front from which liquids could drain. This tray was used for salting large sides of bacon which could be bought more cheaply than rashers.

Most farmers raised their own pigs feeding them on household scraps and small potatoes and supplementing this diet with meal. When the pigs were taken to market one would be kept behind for the farmer's household. This method of pig keeping was also commonly practiced by the farm workers. The farmer would kill his own pig or employ a local butcher to do so, as it was a tricky business. After being caught, the pig might be tied in a 'pig horse'—a contraption which resembled a long wooden bench with handles at each end—to be killed by having its throat cut. Then the whole lot was hung over a dish in a safe place, away from straying animals, so that the blood could be caught. The cook used every part of the pig in various dishes: indeed there was a saying, 'You can eat every part of the pig except for its squeak'.

The bacon would be salted by placing it in the salting tray and turning it daily for a month. After this it would be cut into pieces each weighing approximately 8 lbs. As much salt as possible would be scraped off with a knife and then the bacon would be hung to dry. It could not be eaten for at least a week. Hams were prepared by immersing the meat in a pickle. Large quantities of bacon were consumed at breakfast.

The most impressive piece of furniture in the kitchen was the store-cupboard where the housewife stored all her packeted goods as it was kept warm and dry by the kitchen range.

Here you would see rows and rows of home-made jams, jellies, chutneys and pickles. There would also be tall jars of bottled fruit and vegetables. The reason for this squirrel-like hoarding was to add variety to meals throughout the year. The country cook would not spend good money buying tinned fruit or jars of jam when she was surrounded with an abundance of fruit at those times of the year when they were in season. She would not be in the habit of shopping more than once a week or would have to rely on passing tradesmen. Apart from the economy of preserving any surplus produce for a rainy day, it was very much part of tradition that a well-run household should have a good range of home-made preserves.

| Approximate guide to oven temperatures | | | |
|---|---|---|---|
| Slow | Gas 1–2 | 250–300°F | 145–160°C |
| Moderate | Gas 4 | 350°F | 180°C |
| Hot | Gas 6–7 | 400–425°F | 200–220°C |
| Very Hot | Gas 8–9 | 450–475°F | 230–240°C |

# JAMS

## RHUBARB AND GINGER JAM

*8 lbs. of rhubarb, 8 lbs. of sugar, 4 level teaspoonfuls of ginger, 1 lb. of candied peel.*

Wipe the rhubarb and cut into 1-inch pieces; put in a pan; slightly crush the sugar and spread this over. Leave it until next day and then cut up the lemon peel thinly, add the ginger and boil the whole until it turns a nice red colour, probably $1\frac{1}{2}$ hours. Pour into scalded jars and cover down at once.

*Preserving or granulated sugar may be used in this recipe in place of 'crushed sugar'.*

## PLUM JAM

Take 12 lbs. of good, sound Victoria plums, not over-ripe, and wipe them with a clean cloth. Split and stone them with a silver knife; allow equal weight of crushed preserving sugar. Place the fruit and half the sugar in layers in a deep earthenware bowl, or on large dishes. Let it stand overnight. Next day, boil it up in a preserving pan, stirring carefully. When it begins to be soft, add the rest of the sugar and let it boil until it thickens and sets.

# ELDERFLOWER AND GOOSEBERRY JAM

Take 7 lbs. of gooseberries; 4 heads of elderflower and equal weight of sugar. Top-and-tail the gooseberries and wash them; place the elderflowers, without stalks in a muslin bag, boil both in a little water until soft. Remove the muslin bag and add the sugar. Stir until it is well dissolved, then let it boil rapidly for about 30 minutes, stirring and skimming frequently. Let it cool before covering.

*I would recommend that you do not allow the jam to cool but pot it while it is hot.*

# RASPBERRY JAM

To each lb. of fruit use 1 lb. of sugar. Pick the fruit over carefully, for grubs reside in raspberries when they cannot find loganberries. Put the sugar and fruit into a preserving pan, bring very slowly to the boil, then boil very briskly to setting point. Do not over-boil or the rich ruby thickens to brown. This is a particularly handsome recipe.

# DRIED APRICOT JAM

Wash 2 lbs. of dried apricots and pour on them 4 quarts of boiling water. Cover and leave for 48 hours. Then simmer gently until the fruit is tender. Add 7 lbs. of sugar. Boil again for 1 hour. Put into pots and cover down at once.

# STRAWBERRY JAM

Pick the stalks from the strawberries and put them in a large copper preserving pan. Mash them with your spaddle to break them as much as you can. Put them over the fire, making them quite hot, almost to the boil. Pass them through a very fine colander. Boil the strawberries again for 20 minutes, stirring them all the time with your spaddle. Weigh them and allow 15 oz. of powdered sugar to every lb. of strawberries. Put in the sugar and boil together, stirring well from the bottom, for ½ an hour over the fire. Fill your pots and place some powdered sugar on the top of them before you put them by. Next day put papers on them.

*I should pot while hot and add the juice and finely grated peel of a lemon to every 3 lbs. of strawberries in order to guarantee a good set.*

# VEGETABLE MARROW PRESERVE

Take 4 lbs. of marrow, peeled, seeded and cut into cubes. Add 4 lbs. of sugar, the juice and shredded rind of 4 lemons, 1 oz. of root ginger, 4 oz. of green ginger and a few grains of cayenne. Place all in an earthen vessel overnight, until the liquid covers the marrow, then boil until the fruit is clear and tender, and the preserve is well set.

*Vegetable marrow makes a very good sweet preserve.*

# GREENGAGE PLUM JAM

Take firm greengages, wipe them with a cloth, stalk them, remove the stones, and weigh the fruit. Set aside an equal weight of sugar and put it on the heat. Crack some of the stones and blanch the kernels and add to the fruit. Place both in a pan with not more than an inch of water. Let it come gradually to boiling, then boil fast for 10 to 12 minutes. Put in the sugar, stirring well until it dissolves and continue to boil fast for 20 minutes. Then place in jars and cover.

# FOUR FRUIT JAM

Take 1 quart of gooseberries, top-and-tail them; add 1 pint of stalked raspberries, 1 quart of picked red-currants and 2 quarts of stoned cherries. Weigh the whole and add 12 oz. of sugar for every lb. of mixed fruit. Boil all together until the jam thickens and sets. Pour off and cover.

## TO PREVENT JAM FROM GOING MOULDY

Cut rounds of tissue paper, the size of the jars. Soak them separately in vinegar and lay close over the top of the jam. Cover in the usual way. Have done this for 3 years and have had no mould.

# CHEESES AND CURD

## APPLE CHEESE

Take some nice large boiling apples, pare and cut them into pieces. To every 6 lbs. of apples add 1 pint of water, 5 lbs. of loaf sugar and the juice and rind of 4 or 5 lemons. Boil the apples with the water until they are soft. Strain them through a colander and then put them with the lemons and sugar into a preserving pan and boil until it jellies.

*'Boiling apples' means cooking apples.*

## LEMON CHEESE

Put $\frac{1}{2}$ lb. of butter, 2 lbs. of sugar, juice of 4 lemons and their grated rind into a big jar and stand this in a pan of boiling water. Stir until the sugar is dissolved. Beat 6 yolks well and add a little by little, stirring continuously. Pot in the usual way. Use for tart-fillings on busy days.

## LEMON CURD

Put $\frac{1}{2}$ lb. of butter in a pan with 4 lemons (grated rind and juice). Add 2 lbs. of sugar and stand in the inner pan of a double cooker to melt and blend. When the sugar is quite dissolved (you must stir from time to time) beat 6 eggs thoroughly and add gradually to the mixture, stirring continuously until it thickens. Bottle down.

# MARMALADES

## APPLE MARMALADE

Take 2 lbs. of good, sound, cooking apples and put them in a lined saucepan with 1 lb. of castor sugar and 1 pint of sweet cider. Let them cook quietly for 3 hours or so, until the fruit is so soft it can be put through a sieve. If it is not sweet enough, more castor sugar can now be added. Put into jars or pots like ordinary jam.

## KATE'S MARMALADE

*One dozen Seville oranges, 6 lbs. of preserving sugar, 1 lemon, 1 quart of water.*

Slice the oranges finely and let them soak overnight in a quart of water. Boil until tender and then add the sugar. Boil 1 hour more and add the juice of 1 lemon before bottling up.

## MEDLAR JELLY

Take fully ripe medlars, peel thinly and slice them removing the pips. Place in a preserving-pan with enough water to cover them. To every 24 medlars allow the juice and thinly-pared rind of $\frac{1}{2}$ a lemon. Boil well until the fruit is thoroughly soft, then strain it through a jelly bag, but DO NOT SQUEEZE IT. Measure the juice, allow a lb. of sugar to every pint and replace it in the pan. Allow about the same amount of lemon juice as before (1 lemon to every 50 medlars) but no more rind. Keep boiling, skimming it well until it sets, probably about $1\frac{1}{2}$ hours. Be careful that the jelly does not stick or burn. This recipe is reputed to equal the best guava jelly.

*Although the medlar has been cultivated in Britain for many centuries it is still not well known. It belongs to the apple family and is not eaten until it appears to be rotten.*

## APPLE JELLY

Rub the apples, cut them up without paring or coring them. Put into a pan and cover with water. Boil 1 hour. Put into a bag and strain. Allow $\frac{3}{4}$ lb. of sugar to 1 pint of juice and boil for 1 hour. Put a little on a saucer and if it jellies, it is done. Pot.

*Apple jelly can be made by using 1 pint of juice to 1lb of sugar and then rapid boiling for 15 to 20 minutes till setting point is reached.*

## SLOE JELLY

To every 2½ lbs. of sloes add 4½ lbs. of cooking apples (which have been chopped but not pared or cored), and pour over 6 pints of water. Boil until all the fruit softens and then strain through a jelly bag. To each pint of juice add 1 lb. of sugar and boil until setting point has been reached.

*Sloes are a wild plum and can be found in the hedgerows in late Autumn. They have a dry sour taste and cannot be eaten raw but make excellent jelly.*

## CRAB APPLE AND ROWAN JELLY

Soak the rowan berries in hot water for a day before you begin. Then add a ⅓ of their weight in chopped crab apples. Simmer fruit with ½ a pint of water to every lb. of fruit. Use the usual jelly procedure with the strained juice. To every pint of uice add a little lemon juice and a lb. of sugar. This astringent jelly is good with meat.

## RED-CURRANT JELLY

Wash 4 lbs. of currants and boil gently in a little water. Strain through a jelly bag. Add a pint of juice to every lb. of heated sugar, bring to the boil and continue to cook for 10 minutes. Pot.

# QUINCE JELLY

Chop the whole fruit into small pieces and place in a preserving pan. Cover with water and simmer until soft. Place through a jelly bag. To each pint of juice add 1 lb. of sugar, and boil to setting point.

*Quinces belong to the pear family and resemble very hard green apples. They make a beautiful red jelly that is a superb accompaniment to meats and poultry. Japonica apples may be used in the same way.*

# BRAMBLE JELLY

To 4 lbs. of blackberries add 2 lbs. of cooking apples, that have been wiped and chopped. Pour over 2 pints of water. Boil over a low heat for 40 minutes. Strain through a jelly bag and weigh. Add 1 lb. of warmed sugar to each pint of juice and boil for 15 minutes. Put into jars.

## THE COVERING OF JARS

As regards covering, opinions vary. Any amount of waxed paper is sold on the market for this job. Bladders are sometimes used or one can use white paper smeared with the white of an egg or dipped in milk. One of the best methods is to cut a piece of paper the size of the jar, nick around the edges for a better fit and then soak it in brandy or whisky. Make an outer covering from vegetable parchment tin or paraffin paper and tie this firm and fast'

Sealing wax may be employed for covering corks or bottled fruit as it renders them more air-tight.

When using bladders
Wash them in warm water, partly dry them and stretch them, while damp, over the top of the jar as tightly as possible. Tie with string. These will dry quite hard and will be absolutely airtight. One bladder should cover four or five jars. A small round of white paper should be put on top of the contents before the bladder is put on. These bladder covers can be used again if they are carefully removed from the pots when they are opened. Untie the string and then just hold a warm, damp cloth over the bladder for a few minutes until the skin softens. It can then be removed without cutting. Note: Always use bladders for tying down pickles.

*The cook must have blessed the day when she was able to buy packets of cellophane covers!*

# CHUTNEYS

## GREEN TOMATO CHUTNEY

Wash and dry 2 lbs. of green tomatoes, cut into thick slices. Put in a bowl with 2 sliced onions, a tablespoonful of salt and leave for 12 hours. Pour off a little of the liquid from the bowl and mix with a teaspoonful of dried mustard and a teaspoonful of ginger. Put everything in a pan with 6 oz. of moist sugar, 4 oz. of raisins and a pinch of cayenne pepper. Stir well with a wooden spoon, simmering gently to a jam consistency. Pot in the usual way.

# APPLE AND MARROW CHUTNEY

Cut 8 lbs. of marrow into small cubes. Sprinkle with salt and leave overnight. Drain well. Peel and core 4 lbs. of cooking apples and place in a large preserving pan with the marrow, 2 lbs. of sliced onion, 3 lbs. of sugar, 4 pints of vinegar, 1 teaspoonful of paprika, a little salt and an oz. of pickling spices tied in a muslin bag. Cook over a slow heat until it thickens and then pot.

*When preparing the marrow remove the skin and pips.*

# PICKLES

## MRS. HYDE'S INDIAN PICKLE

*1 gallon of vinegar, ¼ lb. eschalots, ¼ lb. flour mustard, ¼ lb. salt, 2 ozs. mustard seed, 2 oz. tumeric, 1 oz. black pepper (ground fine), 1 oz. cayenne.*

Mix all the ingredients well together. Add cauliflower sprigs, radish pods, cucumber, onions, capsicum pods, nasturtium seeds, small unripe tomatoes or any other vegetables as they come into season, except for red cabbage or beetroot. Stir every day after adding fresh vegetables. Do not boil the vinegar and be sure to wipe and dry the vegetables before you use them.

*'Eschalots' are shallots or spring onions and 'flour mustard' means mustard powder.*

# PICCALILLI

Take pieces of cauliflower sprigs, sliced white cabbage, chopped celery, sliced radish and a few elderflowers. Salt for 2 to 3 days. Drain, mix with chopped apple and cucumber slices. Spice vinegar with tumeric, ginger, garlic and bruised mustard seed. Put into jars and pour on the strong vinegar.

# HOT PICKLE (GOOD)

To a gallon of the best vinegar add about 2 oz. of ginger, peppercorns, mustard seeds, cayenne, a little mace, a very few cloves and some capsicums, horseradish and tumeric. Salt the vegetables and dry them for 3 or 4 days. Pour boiling vinegar over them and let them remain 3 weeks, strain off the vinegar and add more in the same way. Let it remain a fortnight. Then boil the vinegar again and throw over the potted vegetables.

*The 'best vinegar' is white vinegar and not malt.*

# TOMATO SAUCE (KEEPING)

Cut up 6 lbs. of ripe but not over-ripe tomatoes. Cook gently, rub pulp through a sieve and return it to the pan with $\frac{1}{2}$ lb. of finely chopped onion, 1 oz. chopped shallot, $\frac{1}{2}$ lb. sugar, $\frac{1}{2}$ oz. salt, $\frac{1}{4}$ oz. mixed spice, $\frac{1}{2}$ pint vinegar and a little pepper. Boil all together slowly until sauce thickens. Pour into heated bottles and seal at once. You may sterilize the filled bottles and I very much recommend this.

## MILITARY PICKLE

To each gallon of cold vinegar add ½ lb. of mustard, 4 oz. tumeric, 2 oz. curry powder, a handful of salt and ½ a teaspoonful of grated nutmeg. Boil all together and let the liquid cool. Boil or scald the vegetables with the vinegar, adding a little garlic and some small onions. Put them in a jar and pour over the pickle. The following vegetables may be used: gerkins, cauliflowers, cucumbers, a little sliced mango, preserved ginger-root, and a few slices of angelica root. This pickle will be ready for use about 3 weeks after it is made.

## PICKLED CUCUMBERS

Rub the cucumbers well in salt and keep them covered in salt for 2 days, turning over occasionally. Rinse and drain thoroughly. Place in a large jar which has been lined with vine leaves, reserving some to cover over the top of the jar. Boil together 1 pint of vinegar and 3 pints of water and pour over the cucumbers. A few hours later boil together 1 pint of vinegar and 2 pints of water and having poured off the first lot, pour over the stronger vinegar solution. Next day pack the cucumbers in jars and boil some fresh vinegar with a little garlic, some allspice berries, peppercorns, bay-leaves, a few sprigs of thyme and mace. A little sugar may be added if desired. Cool the vinegar and pour over the cucumbers. Cover with vine leaves and cork down. If liked they may be packed in a sweeter vinegar.

*It is better to use cucumbers in the 'gherkin' stage.*

# PICKLED BEETROOT

This is an excellent stand-by for salads when good beetroot is unobtainable. Choose young dark-coloured beetroots, wash them well being careful not to bruise the skins. Do not cut off the rootlets and leave on a few inches of the stalks. Drop into boiling water and cook until amost tender. Allow to cool and remove skins and roots. Either cut into slices or leave whole as required, and pack into jars. Boil together the following: 1 quart of vinegar, or enough to cover the beetroot, a little whole pepper, a few allspice berries, some bruised whole ginger, a few cloves, a blade of mace and 1 tablespoonful of sugar. Allow to cool and add 1 tablespoonful of grated horseradish, if you like, and cover the beetroots. Scrape a little horseradish on top of each jar and seal down.

*This recipe sounds marvellous but covering the beetroot with spiced vinegar will preserve them as well.*

# PICKLED SHALLOTS

Peel the shallots and cover with brine made from 1 lb. of salt to 8 pints of water. Leave 2 days. Drain, pack into jars, and cover with heavily spiced cold brown vinegar. This recipe is best when the shallots are young.

*Some people boil the spiced vinegar and pour it over the onions while still hot. I do not recommend this method as the onions become very soft.*

## PICKLED RED CABBAGE

The cabbage is best after a slight frost, as then it is hard and firm. Take off outer leaves and shred inner part finely. Put into a dish, cover with salt and let it stand 24 hours. Drain well and put into jars. Boil 1 quart of vinegar with 1 to 1½ oz. spice (tied in a muslin bag). When vinegar is cold pour over the cabbage and cork tightly.

## PICKLED WALNUTS

Gather some 'green' walnuts (usually available in June), that are surrounded by a green husk. Test they are young by passing a needle through them. Place the walnuts in a large bowl and cover with a brine using 2 lbs. of salt to 4 pints of water. Make sure they are under this brine by placing a plate on top. Leave for 9 days. Remove the walnuts and drain well. Place on trays and leave them to dry outside in the sun, until they are a shiny black. This will take 3 days depending on the weather. Place the dried walnuts in jars and pour over hot spiced vinegar. Fasten down well. They can be eaten at the end of a month but are better after 6 months. They will keep good for 2 to 3 years.

# TO PICKLE EGGS

Boil 8 eggs for 12 minutes and then place them in cold running water. Remove the shells and place the eggs in jars. Boil a pint of spiced vinegar and pour over the eggs while still hot. When cold tie them down with a bladder to exclude the air. This pickle will be ready for use after a month. Use eggs when they are cheap and plentiful.

## GENERAL RULE FOR BOTTLING

New rubber rings must always be used. Only perfectly sound, high-grade, clean fruit should be used for bottling. Syrup or water should be absolutely boiling when poured over the fruit and must well cover it. Choose fruit of even size, which may be left whole or cut in halves according to the shape of the jars. Pack the fruit very tightly, using a smooth wooden stick to assist the packing, rather than a metal spoon which might damage the fruit.

The syrup

The syrup in which the fruit is preserved may be of any desired strength. To make it dissolve 4 to 6 oz. of sugar in a pint of water and simmer gently for 10 minutes. Allow it to become quite cool and strain it through a piece of clean muslin. Reheat before pouring over the fruit. If the syrup is boiled longer it becomes heavier, because of the evaporation of the water.

# THE METHOD OF BOTTLING

Fill the jars with fruit or vegetables and pour on the boiling water or syrup to the top of the bottles. Place rubber rings and screw caps on loosely. Stand on a thick cardboard or asbestos mat on the middle shelf of the oven. Space must be left between the bottles which of course must not overlap the mat. Cook until fruit is tender. The cooking time will vary according to the type and ripeness of the fruit and the size of the jars. Here is a general cooking guide:

30 to 35 minutes for strawberries, raspberries, loganberries, ripe plums, gooseberries, tomatoes, rhubarb.

40 to 45 minutes for apricots, peaches (soft variety), firm plums, greengages, damsons, cherries.

50 to 60 minutes for black- and red-currants, pears, hard yellow-fleshed peaches.

60 minutes or longer for winter pears and quinces if a deeper colour is desired.

When the fruit is cooked, lift the jars on to a thick, slightly damp cloth. Have ready extra boiling syrup, and add enough to each jar of fruit to overflow. If fruit is being bottled in water, add boiling water. Immediately screw down caps tightly. When cold, test jars with glass tops by removing the screw cap and lifting each by its glass top. If the glass top does not come away, the bottle is satisfactorily sealed. Wipe down the jars and store in a dry, cool, dark place. Bottled fruit should keep indefinitely if the foregoing instructions are carefully followed and good air-tight containers are used.

# DRYING, CANDYING AND CRYSTALLIZING FRUIT

## DRIED APPLE AND PEAR RINGS

Core fruit, peel thinly and cut into rings as thick as a Victorian wedding ring. Steep them in a brine made from $1\frac{1}{2}$ oz. of salt to 6 pints of water, for 10 minutes. Thread rings on rods or sticks of wood that fit across the width of the oven. Dry very slowly to a leathery consistency, turning them occasionally.

## CANDIED PEEL

Remove all the white pith from tidy halves of orange, lemon or grapefruit peel, soak for 16 hours in salt water, then rinse under the tap until all saltiness and bitterness has vanished. Make a syrup, using 1 pint of water to 1 lb. of sugar, and cook the peels in it until soft but not broken. Drain them, restoring liquor to pan, and add another lb. of sugar to each pint of liquor, boiling this until it is a thick soup. In go the drained peels and they boil on gently until the sugar flakes off the spoon. Dry the peels on a warm hob with plenty of crystallized sugar left in the hollows. They are best stored in nests of crushed paper.

# CRYSTALLIZED ANGELICA STALKS

Choose young stems—April stems are best—cut into pieces about 4 inches long, boil until tender. Some people soak them in boiling brine as a preliminary. Strip off outer skin then return to the pan for a second boiling. Stems will now be bright green and ready for candying. Weigh and allow 1 lb. of sugar to a lb. of angelica stems. Place in an earthenware crock, coat with sugar, and leave for 2 days. Then boil all well together. Remove the angelica. Add to the syrup another handful of sugar and once more boil the angelica in the syrup for about 7 minutes. Drain, dry in a cool oven with the door open.

# CRYSTALLIZED CHESTNUTS (MARRONS GLACÉS)

Take large sound nuts, shell and blanch them in boiling water until a needle will go into them easily. Take off the skin, and place each nut in warm water with a little lemon juice. Have ready a plain syrup made with 2 parts sugar to 1 of water. Drain the chestnuts, and put them in the syrup, let them boil very slowly until they are quite tender but not broken. Remove and drain in a sieve and boil the syrup to 'crack' and let it become nearly cold. Dip in the chestnuts one by one on a long knitting needle. Let them become thoroughly coated, and dry them off in the oven or on a rack.

# CRYSTALLIZED VIOLETS

Cut off the stem close to the 'spur' and shake the flowers free of dust or tiny insects. Make a white sugar syrup and boil the flower heads in it several times, cooling completely between each boiling, until finally the syrup candies and the petals are quite transparent. Sprinkle with fine sugar and store in boxes with plenty of paper. This recipe may be used to crystallize other small flowers or petals.

# CURING

## CURING HAMS

*For 2 hams weighing 16 to 18 lbs. each you will need 1 lb. of moist sugar, 1 lb. of common salt, 2 oz. saltpetre and a quart of good vinegar.*

As soon as the pig is cold enough to be cut up, take the 2 hams and rub them well with salt, and leave in a large pan for 3 days. When the salt has drawn out all the blood, drain and throw the brine away. Mix the sugar, salt and saltpetre together in the above proportion, rub the hams well with this. Put them in a large vessel and keep salt over them. Let them remain 3 days and then pour a quart of good vinegar over them. Turn them in the brine every day for a month, then drain them well and rub them with bran. Have them smoked over a wood fire, and be particular that the hams are hung as high as possible from the fire; otherwise the fat will melt and they will become dry and hard.

# PICKLE FOR A TONGUE

*¾ lb. common salt, 3 oz. saltpetre, 1 lb. of golden syrup (or better still common treacle).*

Trim the root of the tongue and leave a little of the fat. Place the tongue in a deep dish, cover with salt and let it lie until the next day. Pour off the slime that will come from it and rub well with the pickle. Turn and rub it every day for a week. Renew the pickle and turn and rub for another week. It is then ready for use. Tongues are always best when used straight from the pickle. If this is not convenient, however, they should be taken out, rubbed dry and hung up to keep or smoked if preferred.

Another pickle for a tongue using the above method is made from ¾ lb. common salt, 3 oz. saltpetre, ¾ lb. brown sugar.

# BATH CHAP (Pig's Cheek)

Remove cheeks from the head and clean them well. Take out the bone, cover flesh with common salt and leave cheek to drain overnight. Next day rub well, using extra salt and a little coarse brown sugar mixed together. Cover the cheek with this mixture and leave for 12 days, turning daily. Do not use any saltpetre when curing Bath Chaps, otherwise the flesh will be too hard.

# WEST COUNTRY METHOD OF CURING HAMS

Take 3 or 4 hams weighing 14 or 16 lbs. each. Let them hang for a day, then rub well into each one 2 oz. of sal prunella, 2 oz. of saltpetre and a lb. of salt. Put the hams into a deep pan and rub them each day for 3 days. Make a pickle by boiling together 3 gallons of water, 4 lbs. of common salt, 4 lbs. of bay salt and 7 lbs. of moist sugar. Skim thoroughly and when the pickle has boiled for 20 minutes, pour it hot over the meat. The hams must be rubbed and turned daily and their relative position altered, the one on top being put to the bottom and so on. At the end of 3 weeks they must be drained, dried and smoked.

This pickle will be found excellent for beef, tongues, bacon, etc. It will keep for several months if it is boiled and skimmed each time it is used. It should be kept closely corked. Salt and treacle should be added to make up the strength that is evaporated.

*Bay salt is large crystals made from two kinds of salt. One is prepared by evaporation from sea-water and the other by evaporation from salt springs and lakes. Saltpetre is used to redden the meat. Sal prunella is a preparation of fused nitre.*

# A TIP ON KEEPING HOME-CURED BACON AND HAM

It is wisest to dust with ginger and black pepper before hanging as this keeps the flies away, and then tie it in muslin or calico.

# A LARDER MISCELLANY

## TO KEEP EGGS FOR THE WINTER

Take a large stew pot or bowl and put a layer of common salt in the bottom. Then insert the eggs with the thin end downwards, and in such a way that they do not touch each other. Then put another layer of salt on the top and repeat the process until the pot is filled, having salt as the top layer. Tie down very tightly and whenever an egg is taken out take care to tie down again. Be sure the eggs are fresh and have not been much shaken. They will keep good for months. Water-glass is sometimes preferred.

Other methods
Using water-glass in tubs, crocks or galvanized pails. Test the eggs carefully before preserving. Do not leave them more than 24 hours before preserving but make sure the egg has cooled. Keep the preserving jars or pails in a cool, airy place.

Submerging in a solution of 1 pint of slack lime, 1 pint salt, 2 oz. of cream of tartar, and 4 gallons of water. Boil all together and skim. Will preserve 150 eggs.

# THE SALTING OF BEANS

Only use young French beans, or runner beans. Cut around each bean removing the tough outer edge. Slice them. Put a layer of common salt in a jar and place a layer of beans on top. Repeat until the jar is full ending with a layer of salt. Seal well. Keep in a dark cupboard or wrap some brown paper around the outside of each jar. When you come to use them, wash them well in plenty of water.

*Do not allow the beans to soak overnight in water as they will absorb the salt. Table salt is not suitable.*

# DRYING OF HERBS

The general rule is to harvest herbs when buds are just turning to flowers. July is the month for tarragon and thyme, August for basil, mint, sage, pennyroyal, marjoram, lemon balm, savory and chervil. The aim is to cull the plants while the essential oil content is high. Cut on a cool dry morning and spread the clean stems on paper. Dry in an attic, a cool oven with the door open or outside covered with thin muslin. They can also be hung in bunches in paper bags. Avoid dampness that causes mould or strong sunlight that drives out the oils. Beware of dust. When herbs are truly dry, rub them through a sieve and store in dry jars. If the jars start to must over, remove the herbs and complete drying. Label all jars.

# TO PRESERVE LEMON JUICE

Strain juice through muslin and fill small screw-top jars with it to within half an inch of the top. Cork or screw jars as soon as you have put $\frac{1}{2}$ a teaspoonful of sweet oil on the top of each. Store in a cool place. When you require one of the small jars, wind cotton wool round an orange stick or skewer and draw off the oil. The juice will be untainted.

## CHOCOLATE LEAVES

Collect clean rose leaves that are perfect in shape with a little stalk on them. Do not wash. Melt some cooking chocolate in a basin over hot water and dip the underside of the leaf in it. Do not immerse the whole leaf. Allow the chocolate to harden. Very carefully peel off the rose leaf and store the chocolate leaf in a dry air-tight box. Use for decorating cakes and desserts.

## ROSEHIP SYRUP

Pick bright orange hips, crush and put into boiling water ($1\frac{1}{2}$ pints per lb.). Bring back to the boil, stand for 15 minutes, strain through muslin. Bring solid mass to boil again in $\frac{1}{2}$ pint of water, stand again for 15 minutes and strain. Mix juices, reduce by slow boiling to a pint per lb. Sweeten and bottle. Do not keep too long.

# Baking day: bread, cakes and biscuits

Baking day was one of Granny's busiest days. She started by making the bread dough which she would leave to rise in a large bowl, nestling in the warmth of her range. She then set to work making cakes and rolling pastry into various shapes. The bread was then ready for kneading and once it had been shaped it was returned to the warmth to double in size. In order to bake the loaves the range had to be well stocked with fuel so that it produced a great heat.

Tea time on a farm was usually between five and six o'clock, after the cows had been milked and the chores completed. It was a meal of bread and butter with home-made jam and a few cakes. Rarely was a hot dish served.

A farmer's wife often held tea parties to which she invited her farming friends with their children. They would arrive about three o'clock and leave just before five, in time to return home and get their own family's tea. It was a chance for the hostess to display her best china and dainty tea knives on a neatly embroidered table cloth. The whole setting was completed with a small bowl of flowers. A 'well run' tea party would include sandwiches or thinly sliced bread and butter served with home-made jam. There would be scones, and it was an unwritten rule that five different varieties of cakes were also served. There would be a fruit cake, a sponge, some small cakes (which might include meringues and éclairs), biscuits and an iced cake or gateau.

As a child I can well remember attending tea parties given by my aunt. I used to look forward to them immensely and loved that magic moment when we were ushered into her dining room and saw the beautiful spread. We were also expected to be on our best behaviour and started our tea with bread and butter. We had to wait to have the cakes passed and on no account were we to help ourselves. Even in a young child's eye tea parties were a slightly formal occasion, although held in an extremely relaxed and friendly atmosphere.

# BREADS, SCONES AND TEABREADS

## TEA SCONES

½ *lb. flour, 1 teaspoonful of baking powder, 1 egg, milk to mix (about a gill), 1 oz. butter or margarine.*

Sieve the flour with the baking powder. Rub the fat into the flour, mix all these ingredients together. Beat the egg and add to the flour, etc. Add sufficient milk to make a soft but not too sticky dough. Flour the board, roll out the mixture until it is about half an inch thick. Cut scones into rounds with a plain cutter. Place on a greased baking-sheet. Brush scones with milk. Bake in a hot oven for about 10 to 15 minutes. Slit open and spread with butter. You can vary this recipe by adding a small quantity of sugar and fruit to make them into sweet scones.

# SALLY LUNN TEA CAKES

Mix ½ a teaspoonful of salt in 1 lb. of flour and add 3 tablespoonfuls of sugar. Melt a ½ oz. of butter into ½ a pint of new milk. When milk is warm pour it over ½ oz. of compressed yeast. Add a little well beaten egg and a little grated nutmeg. Stir lightly into the flour with a wooden spoon, cover with a cloth and set in a warm place to rise. Knead on a floured board, place in tins and allow to rise again. Bake in a hot oven for 15 to 20 minutes.

*The tea cakes are usually 3 to 4 inches in diameter. They are best split in two then toasted and served with cream and jam.*

# BREAD

*1¾ lbs. of household flour, 1½ teaspoonfuls of salt, ½ oz. of compressed yeast, ¾ pint of tepid water.*

Warm a large basin and the flour. Mix the salt with the flour. Make a well in the centre. Cream the yeast in another warm basin, with a wooden spoon, gradually stirring the tepid water into it. Pour this in the middle of the flour, work a little of the flour into it and sprinkle some on top. Cover the basin with a cloth and put it in a warm place for the mixture to rise for 20 minutes. Then work the whole into a dough and knead well on a board. Flour the basin, and return the dough to it. Cut a cross on the top, cover and again set in a warm place for 1½ hours. Knead the dough again lightly, shape it into loaves and put into greased, floured bread tins or baking trays. Prick the top with a fork or mark a cross with a knife and put in a warm place to prove for half an hour. Bake in a hot oven for 1 hour. To test whether the loaf is done: tap the bottom and if it sounds hollow it is sufficiently baked.

*When making bread always use strong flour. Compressed yeast is dried yeast.*

## SCOTCH SCONES

*1 lb. flour, ¼ teaspoonful of bicarbonate of soda, 1 teaspoonful of baking powder, pinch of salt, enough buttermilk or fresh milk to mix to a dough that can be easily handled.*

Mix all together and roll out, cut in triangles or rounds and cook on a greased griddle or frying pan.

## HOT TEA CAKES

Mix ½ lb. of flour, 2 or 3 eggs, sugar, (nutmeg if approved) and a little barm. Should the eggs be not sufficient to wet it add a little milk. Put it into your tin and let it rise before the fire for half an hour before baking. It will take about half an hour to bake. Either divide into half and put butter enough to soak it through or cut into thin slices and butter it as you would hot toast.

*Barm is yeast rising on fermented malt liquors.*

# WALNUT LOAF

*9 oz. self-raising flour, 2 tablespoonfuls golden syrup,
1 oz. butter, 3 oz. castor sugar, 4 oz. sultanas,
2 oz. walnuts, 1 egg, ½ cupful milk, good pinch of salt.*

Sift the flour into a basin, rub in the butter and
add all the dry ingredients. Mix with the syrup,
warm milk and well beaten egg. Put into a greased
bread tin and allow to stand for 20 minutes. Bake
in the roasting oven at a very moderate temperature
for 1 to 1½ hours.

# LARGE CAKES

## SEED CAKE

*1 lb. flour, ½ lb. margarine or 6 oz. dripping, 2 oz.
candied peel, ¼ teaspoonful of bicarbonate of soda,
7 oz. castor sugar, milk to mix (about 1½ gills), 2 eggs,
1 oz. caraway seeds.*

Grease and line a tin. Sieve the flour with the
bicarbonate of soda in a large basin. Rub the fat
into the flour. Cut the peel into very small pieces
and add to the flour with the rest of the dried
ingredients. Beat the eggs well and mix with the
milk. Add both to the mixture. Place the mixture
in the tin and bake in a moderately hot oven for 1½
hours.

# SAND CAKE

*¾ lb. cornflour, 8 oz. castor sugar, 7 oz. margarine, 1½ teaspoonfuls baking powder, lemon or vanilla flavouring, 3 eggs, milk (if required).*

Grease an oblong or round cake-tin and line with greased paper. The latter should reach just above the top of the tin. Sieve the cornflour and measure out about 1 tablespoonful. Mix with the baking powder and set aside. Separate the yolks from the whites of the eggs. Beat the sugar and fat to a cream. Beat up the yolks and stir half into the creamed fat and sugar. Beat for 5 minutes. Then add the remaining yolks and beat well again. Fold the cornflour in lightly. Then add the stiffly-beaten egg whites. Flavour with the vanilla or lemon and mix thoroughly. Lastly add the baking powder and stir it in with the other ingredients. Put into the tin and cook in a moderately hot oven for ¾ hour. When lightly brown cover top with a paper.

# CHOCOLATE CAKE

Take ½ lb. of butter and beat it to a cream with ½ lb. of powder sugar. Add 7 egg yolks, ½ lb. of vanilla chocolate (grated), 4 oz. of flour, 4 oz. of ground almonds and ⅓ a teaspoonful of baking powder. Whisk the egg whites until stiff and stir lightly into the mixture. Bake in a flat tin for 20 to 30 minutes in a moderate oven. When cold ice over and cut into fancy shapes.

*Powder sugar is castor sugar.*

# DELICIOUS CAKE

*¼ lb. butter, ¼ lb. castor sugar, 3 eggs, ½ lb. flour, ½ teaspoonful bicarbonate of soda, 1 teaspoonful cream of tartar, 3 drops vanilla essence.*

Mix all the ingredients well together. Bake in a moderate oven for about ¾ to 1 hour. Grated orange or lemon rind may be added.

# THICK GINGERBREAD

*1 lb. treacle, ¼ lb. butter, ¼ lb. brown sugar, 1½ lbs. flour, 1 oz. ground ginger, ½ oz. allspice, 1 teaspoonful of bicarbonate of soda, 3 eggs, ¼ pint warm milk.*

Mix together flour, sugar, ginger and spice. Add the warmed butter. Mix in the treacle and well beaten eggs. Warm the milk, mix with the soda and stir thoroughly into the mixture. Place in a greased tin and bake in a moderate oven for ¾ hour.

# A POUND CAKE

*1 lb. of flour, 1 lb. of currants (some caraways if preferred), ½ lb. of sugar, 8 eggs, and 1 lb. of butter.*

Let it be well beaten for an hour, and be put in the oven directly it has been put in the tin. 1 hour will bake it.

# SULTANA CAKE

*1 lb. flour, 6 oz. sugar, 3 eggs, ½ lb. margarine or butter, 2 teaspoonfuls of baking powder, milk to mix (about 1 gill), ½ lb. sultanas, 1 lemon (grated rind), 2 oz. candied peel.*

Wash and dry the sultanas. Prepare a cake tin by greasing it. Cream the fat and sugar together. Cut the peel into small pieces and remove the stalks from the sultanas. Sieve the flour and baking powder into a large bowl, add the lemon rind. Beat the eggs separately and add to the creamed mixture. Stir in the flour, sultanas and peel. Mix well adding a little milk if required. Put into the prepared tin and bake in a moderate oven for 1½ hours.

# ECONOMICAL CAKE

*½ lb. flour, 1 teaspoonful of mixed spice, 4 oz. sultanas, 1 teaspoonful of cream of tartar, ¼ flat teaspoonful bicarbonate of soda, 2 teaspoonfuls vinegar, ¼ lb. margarine, ¼ lb. sugar, about 1 gill of water.*

Grease a small round cake-tin and line with greased paper. The latter should reach 2 ins. above the top of the tin. Sieve together the flour, soda, spice and cream of tartar. Rub in the margarine until it is like breadcrumbs. Add the sugar and sultanas and mix together. Add the vinegar and sufficient water to form a paste but be careful not to make the mixture too moist. Beat up thoroughly for 5 minutes. Place in the prepared tin and bake in a moderately hot oven for about 45 minutes. Turn on to a sieve and leave until cold.

## MADEIRA CAKE

*6 oz. self-raising flour, 3 oz. butter, 4½ oz. castor sugar, 2 to 3 eggs, little grated lemon rind, 1 to 2 slices citron peel.*

Cream the butter and sugar together until white, and add the eggs one at a time, beating each one well in. Stir in the flour and lemon rind lightly, put in a prepared tin and bake for about 1¼ hours. Arrange the citron peel on top about half way through the cooking time.

## DUNDEE CAKE

*9 oz. flour, 8 oz. sultanas, 8 oz. castor sugar, 8 oz. butter, 2 oz. ground almonds, 2 oz. whole almonds, 8 oz. currants, 1 teaspoonful baking powder, 4 eggs, 2 oz. cherries, pinch of salt.*

Cream the butter and sugar well together, add the eggs one at a time, beating well, then add fruit and lastly flour and baking powder sifted together and the ground almonds. Place in a prepared tin and cover the top with split almonds. Cook in a slow oven for 2 hours.

## BOILED FRUIT CAKE

Put into a saucepan 1 teacup of sugar (or less), 1 teacup of water, 1½ teacups of fruit, ¼ lb. of lard or margarine, 1 teaspoonful of cinnamon, ½ teaspoonful of mixed spice, a pinch of salt, and a little grated nutmeg. Boil together for 3 minutes and then allow to cool. Pour into a mixing bowl. Add 1 teaspoonful of bicarbonate of soda dissolved in a little water and stir in $\frac{1}{2}$ lb. of self-raising flour. Bake in a moderate oven for $1\frac{1}{4}$ to $1\frac{1}{2}$ hours.

## GENOA CAKE

*10 oz. self-raising flour, 4 oz. butter or margarine, 4 oz. castor sugar, 2 oz. almonds, 4 oz. sultanas, 3 eggs or dried eggs, 3 oz. candied peel or angelica, pinch of salt, grated rind of a lemon.*

Blanch and shred the almonds. Clean the sultanas, shred the peel. Cream the butter and sugar, add the eggs one by one, sift the flour and a pinch of salt and stir lightly into the mixture. Add the fruit, grated lemon rind and half the almonds. Pour into a greased tin, lined with greaseproof paper. Sprinkle the rest of the almonds on the top and bake in a hot oven for the first 10 minutes and then place in a cooler part of the oven and bake slowly for 2 hours. Turn out to cool.

## CHERRY CAKE

*8 oz. self-raising flour, 4 oz. butter, 4 oz. castor sugar, 2 eggs, 2 to 4 oz. glacé cherries, 1 to 2 tablespoonfuls of milk, a little grated lemon rind.*

Sieve the flour on to a piece of paper. Cream the butter and sugar together with a wooden spoon until white. Beat in the eggs one at a time, stir in the flour, lemon rind, cherries cut in halves or quarters and milk. Bake in a prepared tin in a moderate oven for from 1 to $1\frac{1}{4}$ hours.

# CHOCOLATE ROLL

*4 oz. self-raising flour, 4 oz. butter, 2 oz. castor sugar, 2 oz. grated chocolate, 2 eggs, 1 tablespoonful of water, vanilla flavouring.*

Melt the chocolate slowly in the water without letting it boil. Sieve the flour. Cream the butter and sugar in a basin with a wooden spoon. Beat in 1 egg with half the flour, beat well, add the other egg and rest of the flour. Beat again thoroughly and flavour gently with vanilla: add the melted chocolate and mix well. Spread on a flat tin lined with buttered paper, letting the mixture be no more than $\frac{1}{4}$ in. thick. Bake in a hot oven until brown and firm. Turn on to a sheet of paper sprinkled with castor sugar. Trim the edges, sprinkle with sugar on top and roll up quickly. Unroll when it is cold, spread with butter-icing and re-roll.

# FARMHOUSE CAKE

*$\frac{1}{2}$ lb. butter, $\frac{1}{2}$ lb. castor sugar, 1 lb. flour, $1\frac{1}{2}$ oz. ground almonds, 6 oz. glacé cherries or raisins, 2 oz. mixed peel, 3 tablespoonfuls of milk, 3 eggs, $\frac{1}{2}$ level teaspoonful bicarbonate of soda, 1 level teaspoonful cream of tartar.*

Cream the butter and sugar together and beat in the eggs one by one. Chop the peel and the cherries finely and add before adding the flour. Add the flour and milk. The mixture should not be too slack. Put into a greased 2 lb. bread tin and bake in a slow oven for $2\frac{1}{2}$ hours.

# SMALL CAKES

## MAIDS OF HONOUR

Blanch, peel and dry 2 oz. of almonds. Put into a mortar with 4 oz. of castor sugar and pound until fine. Add the yolks of 2 eggs, one at a time, mix in 2 tablespoons of cream, 1 tablespoon of orange flower water and $\frac{1}{2}$ oz. of flour. Line some patty pans with pastry, fill with this mixture and bake in a moderate oven for about 20 minutes.

*Orange flower water can be bought at a chemist's.*

## MERINGUES

To every white of egg allow 2 oz. castor sugar. 3 whites of eggs makes 8 complete meringues, (16 sides). Two sides are sandwiched together with thick cream.

Separate the yolks and the whites. Eggs 24 hours old give the best results. Whip the whites with a pinch of salt until they stand up in the bowl. Next fold in half the sugar. Then fold in the rest lightly with a metal spoon. Shape on to greased paper with two tablespoons, which must be kept moist in cold water. Bake in a very cool oven for 2 to 3 hours. It is a good plan to keep the oven door ajar so that the meringues remain white.

*When making meringues leave the whites un-covered in a bowl overnight; they will dry a little and you get better results. Some of my best meringues were made from unfertile eggs that had been in an incubator where they had dried for nearly 30 days.*

[43]

# BRANDY SNAPS

*2 oz. butter, 2 oz. plain flour, 2 oz. sugar, 2 oz. golden syrup, ½ teaspoonful of ground ginger, 1 teaspoonful of brandy.*

Melt the fat with the sugar and syrup in a saucepan. Add the flour, ginger and brandy. Grease a flat baking tray and place teaspoonfuls of the mixture on it. Bake for 8 to 10 minutes in a moderate oven. Remove and allow to cool a little before wrapping around a greased wooden spoon. They can also be served flat.

# FAIRY BASKETS

*3 oz. butter, 4 oz. castor sugar, 6 oz. self-raising flour, 2 eggs, 2 oz. coconut, ¼ pint thick cream, a little jam, angelica.*

Cream the butter with the sugar, add the beaten eggs and flour and mix well. Fill some deep patty tins with the mixture and bake for 15 minutes in a fairly hot oven. When the cakes are cold, cut out the centres, spread the outside with a little jam and decorate plentifully with coconut. Fill the centres with jam and place some cream on top. Cut the angelica into strips and arrange to form handles.

# BACHELORS' BUTTONS

To prepare these delicious little cakes rub 2 oz. of butter with 5 oz. of flour, add 5 oz. of white sugar and a beaten egg. Add almond flavouring according to your taste. After mixing well roll them in your hands to the size of a large nut. Sprinkle them with lump sugar and place them on tins with buttered paper. They should be baked lightly.

## VICTORIA BUNS

Line some small patty tins with shortcrust pastry, decorate the edges. Put a small spoonful of raspberry jam in each. Beat 1 oz. butter with $1\frac{1}{2}$ oz. castor sugar. Add 1 egg, 1 tablespoonful of milk, 2 oz. flour, a good teaspoonful of cocoa essence, and $\frac{1}{2}$ a teaspoonful of baking powder. Beat well. Put a small spoonful of this mixture over the jam. Bake in a moderate oven for about 10 minutes.

## GRANNY'S GOOD MIXTURE FOR SMALL CAKES

Whisk 2 eggs for at least 5 minutes. Add $\frac{1}{2}$ a cupful of castor sugar and beat again substituting a wooden spoon for the egg whisk. Add an equal quantity of flour and beat again. Repeat both the sugar and the flour; to the last-named should be added 2 teaspoonfuls of baking powder and a pinch of salt. Bring $\frac{1}{2}$ a cup of milk to the boil and stir in a dessertspoonful of butter. When dissolved pour into the flour mixture and beat thoroughly. Leave for 5 minutes before use. All sorts of dainty cakes can be made from this mixture.

# ÉCLAIRS

*4 oz. plain flour, 2 oz. butter or margarine, ½ pint water (scant), 3 eggs, pinch of salt.*

Bring the butter, water and salt to the boil in a saucepan. Off the heat add the flour and beat well. Add the beaten eggs and mix until there is a smooth paste. Place finger lengths of the mixture on a wet piece of paper. Bake in a hot oven for 15 minutes. Then quickly remove from the oven and split each bun before returning them to the oven to dry out. When cold, fill the buns with thick cream and cover with melted chocolate or coffee icing.

# PRINCESS CAKES

*¼ lb. butter, ¼ lb. castor sugar, 1 egg, 2 oz. ground rice, 2½ oz. flour, 1 teaspoonful of baking powder, a little vanilla flavouring, jam and desiccated coconut.*

Grease a dozen small cake tins. Beat the sugar and butter to a cream. Beat in the egg and mix for 5 minutes. Fold in the flour, ground rice and baking powder. Place a small quantity into each tin, and bake in a hot oven for about 15 minutes. Allow to cool. Put a little jam in the centre of each and sprinkle with coconut. Use red jam for half of them and yellow for the rest. Lift the cakes carefully out of the tins as they are liable to break.

# WINDSOR CAKES

*3 oz. arrowroot, 3 oz. cornflour, 3 oz. flour, 6 oz. butter or margarine, 9 oz. castor sugar, rind of two lemons, 2 eggs, 1½ teaspoonfuls of baking powder, little milk to mix.*

Beat the butter and sugar together, add the eggs gradually and beat well. Stir in the flour, arrowroot, cornflour, ground rice, baking powder and finely grated lemon rind. Add a little milk if required. Put in patty tins and bake in a hot oven for 15 minutes.

# MADELEINES

*2 eggs, 3 oz. flour, 1 oz. margarine or butter, ½ teaspoonful of baking powder, 2 oz. castor sugar, grated rind of half a lemon, flavouring essence to your taste.*

Break the eggs and whisk with the sugar until thick and creamy. Sieve in the flour, baking powder, melted butter or margarine, lemon rind and flavouring. Mix very well. Put into greased tins and cook in a quick oven for about 12 to 15 minutes. Turn out on to a sieve and when cold brush over with a little jam rubbed through a hair sieve, or with a little dissolved red-currant or crab apple jelly. Sprinkle with desiccated coconut.

## SPICE BUNS

½ lb. flour, ¼ lb. butter or margarine, 2 teaspoonfuls of mixed spice, 1 level teaspoonful of bicarbonate of soda, 4 oz. castor sugar, 2 oz. candied peel, ½ an egg, 1 gill of milk.

Grease 10 small patty tins. Rub the fat into the flour. Add the soda, spice, sugar and peel cut into very small pieces. Beat the egg and mix with the milk. Add both to the dry ingredients and mix well. Place in the tins and bake in a hot oven for 15 minutes.

## BISCUITS

### TO MAKE THIN BISCUITS

Take 1 lb. of flour and 1 lb. of butter, add one glass of brandy, not quite ½ lb. of sugar and 3 eggs. Mix well, roll and cut into small rounds using a wine glass. Bake in a moderate oven until golden.

### MELTING MOMENTS

Melt ½ lb. of butter in a saucepan, allow to cool and then add the following ingredients: 6 oz. plain flour, 2 oz. cornflour, 2 oz. icing sugar and a little vanilla flavouring. Place in teaspoonfuls on a greased tray and bake for 20 minutes in a moderate oven.

## LADIES FINGERS

*4 oz. castor sugar, 2 oz. butter, 4 oz. flour, ½ tea-spoonful of baking powder, ½ teaspoonful of vanilla, 1 egg, milk as required.*

Mix the flour with the baking powder and rub in the butter. Add the rest of the ingredients. Mix well and knead lightly on a floured surface. Roll and cut the pastry into finger lengths. Dredge with castor sugar and bake in a moderate oven for 15 to 20 minutes.

## ALMOND COOKIES

Take 1 cup of butter, ½ cup of white sugar, ½ a cup of brown sugar or 1 cup of white sugar, 2 teaspoon-fuls of almond flavouring, 1 egg, and 2 cups of flour (big). Mix well and roll into small balls and bake in an oven until light brown.

## SHREWSBURY BISCUITS

*4 oz. butter, 4 oz. castor sugar, 8 oz. plain flour, 1 egg, 1 level teaspoonful of lemon rind, pinch of salt.*

Cream the butter with the sugar and add the beaten egg a little at a time. Mix in the flour, salt, and finely grated lemon rind. If too soft place in a cool place to harden. Roll out and cut into rounds. Place on greased baking trays and cook in a slow oven for 15 minutes. When cooling, dredge with castor sugar.

## NAPOLEON BISCUITS

*3 oz. butter, 4 oz. flour, 1 oz. castor sugar, 1 oz. ground almonds, raspberry jam.*

Put all the ingredients, except for the jam, in a bowl and work together. Roll out to $\frac{1}{8}$th inch thickness and cut into finger lengths in pairs to fit. Cook in a cool oven until a pale biscuit colour. Cool, spread one with jam on the under side, fit another on top and sprinkle with icing sugar.

## BUTTER BIRDS

Take 1 cup of white sugar, 1 cup of lard and butter mixed, pinch of salt, 2 eggs, $2\frac{1}{2}$ cups of flour, 1 teaspoonful of vanilla flavouring, and 1 teaspoonful of baking powder. Work all together, then roll into balls the size of a walnut. Press flat on a greased baking tin and place a piece of walnut or cherry in the centre of each. Bake in a moderate oven for 15 minutes.

## RASPBERRY KISSES

*4 oz. castor sugar, 4 oz. plain flour, 4 oz. butter, 4 oz. cornflour, 1 egg, 1 teaspoonful of baking powder, carmine, pinch of salt, raspberry jam, thick cream.*

Cream the butter and sugar together, beat in the egg, sifted flour, cornflour, and baking powder. Add a pinch of salt. Colour a deep pink with carmine. Bake in small balls on a greased baking sheet. When cooked sandwich two together with the cream and raspberry jam.

*Cochineal can be used instead of carmine.*

## OATMEAL BISCUITS

*6 oz. flour, 3 oz. medium oatmeal, 3 oz. castor sugar, 3 oz. butter, ½ teaspoonful of baking powder, 1 egg, little milk.*

Rub the butter lightly into the flour, mix in all the dry ingredients, then add the beaten egg and sufficient milk to form a soft dough. Bake in greased tins or the pastry can be rolled and cut into shapes. Cook in a moderate oven until golden.

## GINGER NUTS OR HUNTING NUTS

*½ lb. flour, 2 oz. butter, 1 oz. brown sugar, ¼ lb. syrup, ½ teaspoonful of salt, ¼ oz. ground ginger, ¼ teaspoonful of allspice, grated rind of one lemon, ½ teaspoonful of bicarbonate of soda.*

Warm the butter and golden syrup together. Add the sifted flour, soda, salt, ginger, sugar and allspice. Mix well and allow to cool. With your fingers roll the mixture into small balls. Place them on a greased baking tray flattening them a little. Bake for 15 minutes in a fairly hot oven.

# Soups and entrées

Lunch was the most important meal of the day for most farmers. Although they had a hearty breakfast they still needed a good mid-day meal. The main course of meat and home-grown vegetables was followed by a simple sweet or pudding. Soup was rarely served. The meat was a joint, poultry, game or offal; a chicken that had finished laying would end up in the pot or the farmer's wife would rear some poultry especially for the table. Some of the cottage dwellers who lived near my grandmother, near the River Parett, used to catch elvers and feed them to their young ducks. Apparently the ducks grew visibly on such delicacies! Game and rabbits were not regarded as a special treat but when one was shot it did provide a change to the menu.

After lunch, which was served at one o'clock, the farmer would have forty winks in his armchair before putting on his boots and starting work again at 2 o'clock. Haymaking sometimes upset this routine and often the farmer's wife would take lunch to the men in the field so as not to hinder the work. Most hay would be made into a haystack in the field and if lunch was brought to him, the farmer would not need to keep travelling home to his farm. After he had eaten his lunch in the field he would have his usual nap before commencing work again.

Any part of the joint or meat left over at lunch would be eaten at suppertime with chutneys and pickles. It was a bonus to the usual bread and cheese.

# SOUPS

## VELVET SOUP

*1 large tablespoonful of butter, 1 tablespoonful of curry powder, 1½ large tablespoonfuls of flour, ½ tablespoonful of rice, 1½ pints of milk or cream, pepper and salt to taste.*

Melt the butter in a pan, add the flour and curry powder and mix to a smooth paste. Then add the milk and bring to the boil. Cook ½ tablespoonful of rice and put it into the soup tureen before pouring in the soup. Serve very hot.

## MUSHROOM SOUP

*1 lb. mushrooms including the stalks, 2 oz. butter, 1 quart of milk, 2 yolks of eggs, a little cornflour.*

Simmer the mushrooms in the milk for 20 minutes and when soft pass through a sieve. Mix the yolks with some of the cooled mixture and stir in the cornflour, pour the rest of the soup over it, add the seasonings and reheat. Do not boil.

## VICTORIA SOUP

Take 1 quart of water, 1 teaspoonful of meat extract mixed with a quart of water OR a quart of cheap stock, 1 lb. of potatoes cut small, ½ lb. of raw tomatoes, sliced raw onion, 1 teaspoonful of salt and a little pepper. Simmer all these for 1 hour and then rub through a sieve.

## MULLIGATAWNY SOUP

*1 quart of beef stock, 1 oz. butter, 2 oz. flour, 4 oz. finely chopped onion, 1 desertspoonful of curry powder, 1 chopped cooking apple, 1 oz. chutney, a little cream, seasoning, 2 oz. boiled plain rice.*

Melt the butter and cook the finely chopped onion. Add the flour and cook for a few minutes. Add the rest of the ingredients except the rice. Cook slowly for 1½ hours. Strain, correct the seasoning and consistency. Add the cream. Serve the rice separately.

## BAKED WINTER SOUP

*1 lb. shin of beef, 2 to 3 sticks of celery, 1 teacupful of lentils, 1 carrot, ½ teacupful of rice, 2 quarts of water, 2 onions, seasonings.*

Wash the lentils and the rice, put them into an earthenware soup pot with the cold water and let them soak whilst preparing the other ingredients. Wipe the meat and cut into small pieces removing any skin. Prepare the vegetables and chop them finely or put them through a mincing machine. Put all into the pot, add seasoning, cover and soak for 1 hour. Then cook in a moderate oven until the vegetables and meat are quite tender, from 2 to 3 hours. Stir the soup occasionally and add more water if necessary. This is very tasty and makes an excellent meal. Serve from the soup pot.

# FISH

## STEWED EELS

*2 lbs. freshwater eels, 1 dozen prunes, 3 teacupfuls of white stock, 2 to 3 small onions, 1 oz. butter, 1 tea-spoonful of lemon juice, 1 oz. flour, 1 teaspoonful of chopped parsley, seasoning.*

Cut the heads off the eels and skin them. To do this, turn back the skin at the top and draw it downwards, turning it inside out. Cut the fish into convenient size pieces and let these lie in salt and water for half an hour or so. Then rinse and drain. Melt the butter in a fireproof casserole, add the flour and the soaked prunes and the stock and season to taste. Lay in the pieces of fish and cover them entirely with the sauce. Place a cover on the casserole and stew slowly by the side of the fire or in an oven until the fish is tender, about 20 minutes. Add the lemon juice and parsley just before serving. A little white or red wine can also be added.

*Eels are also very good if after being prepared in small chunks they are slowly sautéed in butter with a little finely chopped parsley.*

## COD'S HEAD

Take one good sized cod's head and shoulders, washed and cleaned well, put it into a dripping-tin and cover with 2 oz. of butter, broken into pieces and dotted all over. Bake for about 1 hour basting frequently. Lift carefully out of the pan on to a serving dish. Cover with browned breadcrumbs and garnish the dish with plenty of parsley and cut lemon—a few prawns are a great improvement. Strain the liquor from the dripping-tin and add 2 tablespoonfuls of vinegar, a little salt and pepper and a tablespoonful of minced parsley. Heat alltogether and serve with the fish.

*Browned breadcrumbs are fried breadcrumbs.*

## HOW TO COOK ELVERS

Wash the elvers well to remove the frothy substance. Blanch them while still alive in boiling water until they have changed from their transparent appearance to opaque. Strain well. In a large pan melt some butter and then pour in 3 well beaten eggs, (they can be duck eggs), and add a handful of elvers. Gently stir the mixture over a low heat and season well with salt and pepper. Allow the mixture to cook thoroughly, and then serve on hot plates. A little vinegar will enhance this dish.

*Elvers are young eels that have crossed the Atlantic Ocean from the Sargasso Sea to our rivers. They arrive on the spring tides and are especially plentiful on the River Parrett near Stathe where they ride on the bore. They are approximately two inches in length and appear to be transparent except for their eyes. They are caught in large shallow nets from the river banks—usually at night—and are kept alive in buckets filled with river water. Although they are still eaten locally they fetch a good price for export and they are caught by strangers for pin money.*

# FISH MOULD

*½ lb. cooked white fish, 2 oz. butter, 2 tablespoonfuls of breadcrumbs, 3 oz. cold potato, 1 egg, squeeze of lemon juice, seasoning, ½ teaspoonful of anchovy essence, and anchovy sauce made from ½ pint of white sauce mixed with 1 teaspoonful of anchovy essence.*

Remove the bones and skin from the fish and pound well. Mash the potato and add to the fish. Add the breadcrumbs, anchovy essence, lemon juice and seasonings to the fish mixture and mix well. Melt the butter and add to the mixture and finally bind with the egg adding a little milk if required. Put the mixture in a greased pudding basin and steam for 1 to 1½ hours. When ready turn out onto a hot dish and serve with hot anchovy sauce.

# OYSTER PATTIES

*Cases of puff pastry already cooked, 1 teaspoonful of cream, 6 to 8 oysters, 1 yolk of egg, ¼ pint white sauce, few drops of lemon juice.*

Blanch the oysters in their own liquor, strain and remove beards from the oysters and cut into two. To the sauce add salt, cream and lemon juice. Add the oysters, heat carefully and fill the patty cases. Place in an oven to reheat the cases.

# GAME AND POULTRY

It is not given to everyone to be able to afford costly poultry and joints are not appetising in this hot weather. The following will, therefore, appeal to worried housekeepers. Boil a nice rabbit in white stock (however weak it may be) until tender, then put it aside until quite cold. Now have ready some cold tongue cut in dice, some hard-boiled eggs and a little finely-minced parsley. Stuff with this mixture and see you keep it to a nice shape. Place on a dish and pour over the rabbit some thick mayonnaise sauce, garnish with some stars of cucumber and down the centre a sprinkle of coralline pepper. Now put around the dish a nicely-mixed salad and you will have at a small cost a pretty and better still, a good dinner.

*The above was a cutting neatly pasted amongst the handwritten recipes. Coralline pepper is red pepper.*


## QUAILS

Clean, draw and truss as if for a fowl. Brush a little melted butter over the bird, tie a vine leaf over the breast and put a piece of bacon fat over the leaf. Fasten this with a long skewer and arrange several birds on the same skewer. Roast them for 20 to 25 minutes. Remove the bacon and vine leaf and place each bird on a square of buttered toast. Garnish with watercress and serve with fried breadcrumbs and gravy. If no vine leaves are available enclose the birds in a piece of well buttered paper.

# PHEASANTS

Pheasants should always be hung for some days before cooking to acquire the right flavour. In very cold weather 2 or 3 weeks is not too long if liked 'high'. In damp, muggy weather 4 or 5 days is long enough. In old pheasants the spurs are long and sharp, in young ones the reverse. The under beak of most young birds bends easily.

## TO ROAST A PHEASANT

Pluck, draw, singe and truss in the same manner as for a roast fowl. Tie over the breast a slice of fat bacon and cook before a quick fire, basting almost incessantly with butter to prevent it getting dry, otherwise it will be spoilt. When nearly done remove the bacon, dredge with flour and baste well to give it a frothy appearance. Time 30 minutes. Serve with a good gravy, browned crumbs and bread sauce.

*Browned crumbs are fried breadcrumbs.*

## PARTRIDGES AND GROUSE

Choose in the same manner as pheasants. They are dressed, cooked and served in the same way. Time for partridges, about 20 minutes; grouse about 10 minutes longer. Blackcock and ptarmigan are cooked in the same manner as grouse.

# GUINEA FOWLS

May be cooked and dressed in the same manner as pheasants and are a very good substitute for game in the late spring.

## RABBIT STEW

*1 rabbit, ½ lb. bacon, 2 large onions, ½ pint stock, good pinch of mixed herbs, seasoning.*

Cut the rabbit into joints, chop the bacon and slice the onions. In an ovenproof dish place half of the onion with some of the bacon on top of it. Put in the rabbit joints and cover with the remaining onion and bacon. Season well and pour in the stock. Either cook in a moderately hot oven for 2 hours or using a heavy based saucepan cook on top of the hob, checking it regularly.

## ROAST VENISON

The best end of the neck of venison, boned and rolled makes an excellent dish. Venison must be hung for a long time, or it will not be very different from mutton. It should be covered with a thick paste made from flour and water, well basted and roasted until half an hour before it is served, when the paste should be removed and the meat allowed to brown. Venison is very close-grained and needs to be roasted rather slowly and allowance must be made for the paste that covers it. It should be served with a rich port wine sauce.

# JUGGED HARE

Skin and paunch the hare and cut into neat joints, flour them well and fry them brown in 2 oz. of butter. Place them in a stew jar, add an onion stuck with cloves, herbs and peppercorns, a tablespoonful of lemon juice, a pint of stock and 1 glass of port wine. Cover the jar closely and cook gently in a moderate oven for about 3 hours. Thicken the gravy with 1 oz. of flour and 1 oz. of butter mixed together; boil up, season and add the glass of port. Dish the hare in a pile, strain the gravy over, garnish with forceballs. Serve redcurrant jelly with it.

*Force balls are, of course, forcemeat balls.*

# ROOK PIE

*6 breasts of rooks, 8 oz. rump steak, 2 hard-boiled eggs, 2 oz. fat bacon, 2 oz. butter, little brown gravy, pastry, seasoning.*

Place the piece of rump steak in the bottom of a fire-proof dish. Chop the bacon and place on top. Prepare the breasts and place in the pie dish. Dot the butter on top of the breasts and place the chopped eggs in the dish. Cover the whole with the gravy and roll out the pastry and place as a lid. Make sure the pastry has a vent and place in a hot oven for 20 minutes, then lower to a slow oven for another hour.

# PIGEONS

When young the under beak bends easily and the bones each side of the vent are gristle. They can be dressed and cooked in the same way as roast partridges. Time about 20 minutes.

## STEWED PIGEONS

*4 or 5 pigeons, 1 pint of good stock, 1 glass of port wine, 2 shallots, a few mushrooms, 1 teaspoonful of fresh herbs, peel and juice of ½ lemon, 2 oz. butter, 1 tablespoonful of flour, seasoning.*

Cut the pigeons in half, season them well and fry until brown in the butter. Place in a fireproof dish and pour over the stock, port, herbs, lemon peel and juice and finely chopped onions. Cover and cook for 1 hour. Add the mushrooms and a few forcemeat balls and continue to cook for 15 minutes. Will serve 10 portions.

## MAKING OLD FOWLS TENDER

A very old fowl can be made as tender as a chicken in the following manner. Rub the bird first with lemon juice all over, which whitens the flesh and improves the flavour. Then wrap in buttered paper and steam for 2 to 3 hours or longer according to size. The flesh of an old fowl is more nourishing than that of a young one and quite as delicious if cooked like this.

# SQUAB PIE

*Breasts of 3 young pigeons, 1 lb. apples, 8 oz.
chopped onions, 8 oz. shortcrust pastry, ½ teaspoonful
of sugar, seasoning.*

Grease a pie dish, place the onions in it and
sprinkle the sugar on top. Place in the pigeon
breasts and cover with the sliced apples. Season.
Make a pastry lid and cook in a hot oven until the
pastry is set and then lower the heat and cook for
an hour. To prevent the pastry from burning cover
it with a piece of greased paper.

*1½ lbs. lean neck of mutton chops are often sub-
stituted for pigeon breasts nowadays, but the recipe
is still known as Squab Pie.*

## SNIPE AND WOODCOCK

These should be eaten while fresh as they are not
drawn. If stale the throat is moist and muddy.
When young the feet and legs are soft and pliable.
When roasting, truss them by using the beak of
the bird in the same manner as if it were a skewer.
Press the legs close to the body and pass the beak
through the legs and body. The head is skinned
and left on. Hang the birds on a spit feet downwards. Place rounds of buttered toast under the
birds, to catch the trail as it drops—this is con-
sidered a delicacy. Baste the birds constantly with
butter or good dripping. Time, 15 to 25 minutes
according to size.

# MEAT DISHES

## BEEFSTEAK AND KIDNEY PUDDING

*Pastry: 1 lb. flour, 1 teaspoonful of salt, 1 teaspoonful of baking powder, 5 oz. suet, and water to mix to a stiff dough. Roll out and line a basin keeping back a piece for the lid. The rest of the ingredients: 1 lb. good steak, ½ an ox kidney cut up, 1 good teaspoonful of salt, ⅓ teaspoonful of pepper and 2 teaspoonfuls of flour.*

Cut the steak into small thin pieces and beat each well, roll in the seasoned flour and place in the basin. Add the chopped kidney and 2 tablespoonfuls of water, place on the lid and steam for 2 to 2½ hours. Set in an oven for about 10 minutes before turning out. Turn out, cut a small piece out of the top of the lid and pour in boiling water.

## LAMBS' TAIL PIE

Pluck the wool off the lambs' tails or scald them in boiling water in order to make the job easier. Place the tails in a large pot with some root vegetables and simmer until they are tender. Then put them in a pie dish with chopped hard-boiled eggs and parsley. Add a little stock and cover with a pastry lid. Cook in an oven until golden.

*These are the tails that have been docked off young lambs. The modern method is not to cut them off but to bind the tails and let them rot off.*

# A SUMMER STEW

*2 lb. breast of lamb, 1 cos lettuce, 1 cupful each of green peas, young carrots and young turnips, 1 lb. new potatoes, 1 sprig of mint, a few spring onions, a little stock, seasoning.*

Cut the lamb into pieces and season with salt and a little white pepper. Put in an earthenware casserole with the luke-warm stock to cover and bring to the boil. Meanwhile prepare the vegetables; shred the lettuce, shell the peas and cut the other vegetables into small pieces. Remove any scum from the top of the meat, put in the carrot, turnip, onion and lettuce and sprinkle a little more salt on top. Cover and stew for half an hour. Add the potatoes and peas with a sprig of mint and continue to cook for another half an hour or until all is tender. Serve in the casserole.

*You might have to remove some of the surplus grease but this will depend on the leanness of the breasts.*

# FAGGOTS

*1 lb. pig's fry, 8 to 9 oz. white fresh breadcrumbs, 2 oz. fat bacon, 1 small onion finely chopped, pinch of mixed herbs, some caul, seasoning.*

Put the pig's fry, bacon and onion through a mincer followed by the breadcrumbs. Roll the mixture into balls, the size of medium size apples. Place in a meat tin and cover with the caul (which might be supplied with the fry). Bake in a moderate oven for 20 minutes.

# POOR MAN'S GOOSE

*1 lb. liver, 1 large onion, 6 oz. streaky bacon, 3 oz. stuffing made from onion and sage, 2 oz. lard or butter, little flour, seasoning, ½ pint of stock.*

Cut the liver into ½-inch slices and dust with the flour. Melt the fat and fry the liver long enough just to seal it, remove and allow to cool. Place the stuffing on top of the liver and twist the bacon around each slice to secure the stuffing. Place in an ovenproof dish, pour a little of the fat on top and pour the stock around the sides. Cook in a moderate oven for 20 minutes and then remove the lid. Continue to cook for another 10 minutes.

*This recipe is sometimes called ' Mock Goose' and uses heart instead of liver. Then the heart is left whole and stuffed.*

# STUFFED LAMBS' HEARTS

*4 lamb's hearts, 4 oz. butter, 4 oz. forcemeat stuffing, ½ pint stock, seasoning, little flour.*

Clean the hearts and trim them. Fill with the forcemeat and sew up the openings. Heat the butter and sauté the whole hearts in it. Draw away from the fire and braise them very gently for 1½ hours. Baste frequently. When cooked place on a serving dish and add flour to the juices, allow to brown and then stir in the stock. This can be served with the hearts.

*These hearts can be baked in a moderate oven if preferred.*

# BRAWN

*Half a pig's head, $\frac{1}{4}$ teaspoonful of saltpetre, brine (approximately 1 pint of water with 1 teaspoonful of salt), 6 black peppercorns, 2 bay-leaves, 1 blade of mace, 1 carrot, 1 small onion, $\frac{1}{2}$ oz. gelatine, 8 oz. shin of beef.*

Soak the head in brine with the saltpetre overnight. Cut the head minus the ears into pieces and place in a large saucepan, add the seasoning, shin and vegetables. Cover with water and boil for 2 to $2\frac{1}{2}$ hours until the meat is soft. Cut into cubes and place in a 1 lb. bread tin or mould. Reduce the liquor, strain it and add the gelatine. Pour over the meat. Allow to set.

*Make sure the pig's ears have been cleaned of wax. The cooking time in a pressure cooker is 35 minutes.*

# MEAT ROLL

*8 oz. flour, 1 teaspoonful of baking powder, 2 oz. suet, 4 oz. minced beef, 1 small onion, seasoning, water to mix.*

Chop the suet, mix the flour with the baking powder and seasoning. Make to a dough with the water. Roll out into an oblong spread with the minced beef and sprinkle over the very finely chopped onion. Roll up and tie in a scalded floured cloth. Boil for 2 hours. Serve with a good gravy or a tomato sauce.

# STEWED OXTAIL

*1 large oxtail, 4 cloves, 1 large onion, 2 large carrots, salt, ½ teaspoonful of cayenne pepper, 1 oz. flour mixed with 1 oz. butter, chopped parsley.*

Cut the tail into pieces. Place in a large pan and cover with water, bring it to the boil. Skim it well as the scum rises and then add the onion with the cloves stuck in it, the sliced carrots, cayenne, salt and bring back to the boil. Allow to simmer for 2 hours until the meat is tender. Remove the meat and vegetables and keep warm on a serving dish. Add the flour and butter mixture in pieces and cook until it thickens. Pour over the meat and sprinkle on the parsley.

*Make sure all the cloves have been removed.*

## TO PRESS BEEF

Salt a piece of brisket, thin part of the flank or the top of the ribs with salt and saltpetre for 5 days. Then boil it gently with care until it is extremely tender. Put it under a great weight or in a cheese press until perfectly cold.

# VEGETABLES

## STUFFED MARROW

*1 nice sized marrow, ½ lb. minced cooked meat, 2 oz. breadcrumbs, 2 oz. butter or dripping, 1 teaspoonful of mixed herbs, 1 egg, seasoning, little stock.*

Peel and cut the marrow in half, remove the seeds. Mix together the meat, crumbs, herbs and seasoning and add the beaten egg. If very dry add a little stock. Stuff the marrow and tie the halves together. Melt the dripping in a pan, put in the marrow and cook until it is done, approximately 45 minutes, basting often. Make a nice gravy with the juice in the tin and serve with the marrow.

## POTATO RIBBONS

Peel the skins off the potato and then peel round and round very thinly. Let them lie in cold water for an hour, drain and place in a frying basket. Plunge into hot fat. Drain on paper and serve hot.

## PARSNIP SAUCE

Boil 2 parsnips well, when quite tender rub through a sieve. Melt 1 oz. butter, stir in 1 oz. flour and ½ pint of milk, stir until it boils. Add the parsnip pulp, a little salt and pepper and a tablespoonful of cream. Heat up and pour over the fish. Sprinkle with chopped parsley.

# Puddings and cold sweets

The first thing that struck me about Granny's puddings and sweets were the fascinating names: Marguerite Pudding, Parson's Pudding, Queen's Pudding, Nellie's Pudding, etc. Most of the puddings were steamed or cooked in an oven, which, unlike today's ovens, was very economical as the range was available day and night.

Creams were carefully prepared and set in moulds and would grace any table.

## CASTLE PUDDING

Take 2 oz. of butter and add 4 oz. sugar, beat to a cream. Add 2 eggs and 4 oz. flour and beat well again. Add a few drops of almond flavouring and a teaspoonful of baking powder. Grease some small moulds, decorate with cherries or raisins and half fill with the mixture. Steam for 1 hour if in small moulds or 2 hours in larger ones. Serve with wine or raspberry sauce.

Wine sauce: Heat a $\frac{1}{4}$ pint of sherry. Beat up 2 eggs with a tablespoonful of sugar. Add the hot sherry and beat well and pour back into the saucepan. Whisk over a gentle heat until frothy.

Raspberry sauce: Take 2 tablespoonfuls of raspberry jam, $\frac{1}{2}$ pint of water, and a tablespoonful of lemon juice. Boil for 10 minutes and strain. If liked, thicken with a teaspoonful of cornflour mixed in a little water. Boil all up.

# MARGUERITE PUDDING

*¾ lb. flour, 6 oz. margarine, 5 oz. sugar, 1½ tea-spoonfuls of baking powder, 1 egg, 1½ gills of milk, 4 tablespoonfuls of golden syrup.*

Put a saucepan of water on the boil. Grease a pudding basin and put the golden syrup in the bottom of it. Place the flour and baking powder in a basin and rub the margarine into it. Add the sugar and beat well with the other ingredients. Add the beaten egg and milk to the mixture and beat well for a few minutes. Put this mixture into the pudding basin. Cover with greased paper. Put into the pan of boiling water and allow to steam for 2 hours. Turn on to a hot dish and serve.

# BACHELOR'S PUDDING

*4 oz. suet, 4 oz. breadcrumbs, 4 oz. apples, 4 oz. currants, 3 eggs, 2 oz. sugar, juice of a lemon, 4 oz. flour, little nutmeg.*

Chop the apples and suet, add the currants, etc. Beat well and steam or boil for 3 hours.

# HANDFUL PUDDING

A little crumbled bread, the same quantity of suet, raisins, and currants and a little grated lemon rind and sugar. Put in layers and a custard thrown over it.

# A TRIFLE

Lay macaroons and ratafia drops over the bottom of your dish and pour over them as much raisin or white wine as they will absorb; which after they have done pour over them cold custard. It must stand 3 or 4 hours before you put on a thick layer of Italian cream (or preference).

Italian cream: Use a whisk to beat rich cream with the whites of two eggs, little sugar, grated lemon peel and raisin wine.

# TO MAKE CUSTARD

To a quart of raw cream, add the yolks of 6 eggs and the whites of 3. Sweeten to your taste, flavour it with ratafia and bay leaves. Boil it to a proper thickness, when sufficiently cool pour it into your glasses with a little nutmeg grated over.

*A few drops of almond essence can replace the ratafia.*

# PORCUPINE PUDDING

Boil ½ lb. of rice in new milk until perfectly tender but not dry. Then add 6 eggs beaten, a teaspoonful of ratafia, a little lemon rind and as much sugar as shall be sufficient. Mix well and boil in a mould for 1½ hours. Turn it on to a hot dish and stick it thick with almonds split into six. Serve with a rich custard.

# CUSTARD PUDDING

6 eggs and 3 whites, a glass of white wine, grated peel of one lemon and sugar to your taste. Boil 1 laurel leaf in a little milk and add that to the other ingredients. You must rub 2 tablespoonfuls of flour in it. Place in a pint pudding basin and boil for 1½ hours. If not sufficient to fill the basin add cream or milk.

# PARSON'S PUDDING

¼ lb. chopped suet, ½ lb. flour, ¼ lb. currants, ¼ lb. raisins, 1 tablespoonful of moist sugar, ½ teaspoonful of ground ginger, ½ teaspoonful of salt, 2 eggs.

Mix well and boil or steam for 3 hours.

# BAKED MILK FOR FRUIT

Put ½ a pint of milk into a jar and place in a warm oven for 5 to 6 hours, when it should be as thick as rich cream.

# WET NELLY

Soak some breadcrumbs in water for 30 minutes and then add 4 oz. chopped suet, a teaspoonful of mixed spice and 1 oz. sugar. Spoon the mixture into a greased tin and bake for 1½ hours. Cut into squares.

# QUEEN'S PUDDING

Take 4 oz. breadcrumbs and 4 tablespoonfuls of strawberry jam. Place in a pie dish and pour on custard made from 1 egg and 1 pint of milk. Bake in a moderate oven for ½ hour.

# MARLBOROUGH PUDDING

Line a dish with puff pastry and then put a layer of raspberry or any other jam on top of it. Fill the dish with a rich custard and bake.

# IDEAL PUDDING

*½ pint of breadcrumbs, 1 pint of boiling milk, 1 tablespoonful of rennet, grated rind of one lemon, 1 tablespoonful of sugar, 1 oz. butter, yolks and whites of 2 eggs.*

Butter a dish, pour in the mixture and bake until set. Beat the white of eggs and pile on top of the pudding. Place in an oven to brown.

# RASPBERRY CREAMS

To make raspberry creams: take 1½ lbs. cream, add a little raspberry jelly or jam with a little brandy and sherry wine. Sweeten to your taste. Whip it to a light froth with a whisk and fill your glasses.

# RASPBERRY AND APPLE ROLL

Mix ½ lb. chopped apples, 1 oz. sugar, 2 table-spoonfuls of raspberry jam. Make a stiff paste with ½ lb. of flour, 3 oz. suet, a pinch of baking powder and a little salt mixed with cold water. Roll out, wet the edges and spread raspberry and apple mixture over. Roll up and place in a long dish or pie dish that has been greased. Steam for 2 hours. Serve with melted butter or whipped cream.

# PRINCE ALBERT'S PUDDING

Beat to a cream ½ lb. of fresh butter and mix with it by degrees an equal quantity of pounded loaf sugar. Add to these after they have been well beaten, first the yolks and then the whites of 5 eggs which have been thoroughly whisked apart. Then strew lightly in ½ lb. of fresh flour and last of all ½ lb. of raisins weighed after they have been stoned. Put these ingredients, perfectly mixed into a well greased mould and boil for 3 hours. Serve with a wine sauce. The grated rind of a small lemon added to the above is an improvement or candied peel laid rather thickly over the mould after it is buttered.

# GINGER PUDDING

Mix ½ lb. of flour with ¼ lb. of suet, ¼ lb. of moist sugar and 2 large teaspoonfuls of grated root ginger. Place in a greased basin and boil for 3 hours.

# ECONOMICAL FIG PUDDING

Soak 3 oz. of stale breadcrumbs in cold water for an hour. Squeeze well to make as dry as possible. Add 1 egg, 2 oz. of chopped figs cut small, 2 oz. of fine sugar, $1\frac{1}{2}$ oz. of suet, $1\frac{1}{2}$ oz. of flour and a teaspoonful of baking powder. Mix well and steam in a basin for 2 hours. Serve with melted butter.

# JAM ROLY POLY

Roll out $\frac{1}{2}$ lb. of sweet suet pastry into a long strip. Cover well with jam but leave $\frac{1}{2}$ an inch free around the edges. Wet the edges and roll up pinching them well together. Tie in a floured pudding cloth allowing room for it to expand. Boil for $2\frac{1}{2}$ hours. Serve with a custard sauce.

# NELLIE'S PUDDING

*4 oz. self-raising flour, 4 oz. butter, 2 eggs and a white, $3\frac{1}{2}$ oz. fine sugar, plus extra $\frac{1}{2}$ oz., 2 table-spoonfuls of jam.*

Beat the butter with the sugar to a cream with a wooden spoon. Beat in the eggs one at a time. Stir in the flour with a metal spoon. Turn into a buttered dish and bake in a hot oven for $\frac{1}{2}$ an hour. Take out and spread the jam on top. Whisk the egg white until stiff and add $\frac{1}{2}$ oz. of fine sugar, pour on top of the jam. Return to the oven for 5 or 10 minutes, just long enough to colour.

*Fine sugar is castor sugar.*

## SPOTTED DOG

Roll out ½ lb. of sweet suet pastry to an oblong. Lay a handful of raisins on to the pastry leaving a good edge. Dampen this edge and roll up the pastry and pinch the edges well together. Make a pleat in the cloth and tie the ends firmly. Boil or steam for 2½ hours.

*A little lemon rind with the raisins is a great improvement.*

## BLANCMANGE

Simmer the thinly peeled rind of a lemon in a pint of milk and leave for 1 hour. Add 1½ oz. of gelatine to the milk and stir in well. Add 4 tablespoonfuls of sugar and when nearly cool add a pint of good cream and a little brandy. Stir it well and pour into a wetted mould to set.

## EVE'S PUDDING

*4 oz. castor sugar, 1½ lbs. apples (peeled, cored and thinly sliced), 4 oz. butter, 2 eggs, 4 oz. plain flour, 4 oz. sugar, 2 cloves, pinch of salt.*

Cream the castor sugar with the butter and then add the eggs, flour and pinch of salt. Grease an ovenproof dish and place half the apples in it, then add the sugar and cloves and finally cover with the remaining apple. Spoon the creamed mixture on top and bake until set.

# SUMMER PUDDING

Prepare a pudding basin by greasing it with butter. Line it with thin pieces of bread, without their crusts. Take a lb. of berries, either red-currants, blackberries, raspberries or a mixture of any. Sprinkle with sugar and gently heat, with no water, to extract the juices. Pour into the basin. Cover the top of the pudding with more bread and place a saucer on top. Weigh it down well. Leave for 24 hours and then turn out the pudding and serve with cream.

# TRINITY PUDDING

Place $1\frac{1}{2}$ pints of milk with 12 beaten egg yolks, and 2 oz. castor sugar in a double saucepan and slowly cook until it thickens. Pour the custard in a large dish and bake until set. When cool cover with a good layer of sugar and place under a grill until the sugar turns brown and forms a hard crust.

# SYLLABUB

Mix $\frac{1}{2}$ lb. of sugar with the thinly pared rind and juice of 3 lemons. Warm slightly to dissolve the sugar. Whip a pint of cream and add a large glass of wine or a little brandy. Mix both mixtures together and pile into serving dishes.

## BEESTINGS CUSTARD

Take a pint of beesting and put in a pie dish. Add
a pinch of salt and 4 tablespoonfuls of sugar. Stir
well and place in a moderate oven until set.

*Beesting is the milk from a cow that has just
calved.*

## APPLE SNOW

Bake a lb. of cooking apples and beat to a pulp
with a wooden spoon. Add some sugar to taste.
When cold and not too long before serving add 2
well beaten egg whites. Place in glass containers.

*The apples must be pared. One can stew them in a
little water.*

# The home dairy: clotted cream, butter and cheese

Most of the milk from Granny's farm was taken to Langport station and then went by train to the London housewives. Some of the milk was kept on the farm to be made into clotted cream, butter and cheese. My grandmother made butter twice a week, some she used but the major part she took to Bridgwater market. My family's butter was renowned for its superior quality and one baker in Bridgwater always insisted on using it for his Easter biscuits.

In the warm summer months butter was soft on arriving at the market as farmhouses had no form of refrigeration except for cool dairies. My family's butter, however, was always firm. The secret was that the seller used to get up at 4 o'clock on market days and place the butter in the well until she was ready to leave for town. Colouring was not used by my family and in winter the butter was a pale primrose colour but a beautiful buttercup colour in the summer.

The top of the milk would be made into clotted cream and a large pan simmering on the range watched intently by a couple of cats was a common sight. Somerset clotted cream differs from that made in Devonshire as the milk is not separated and hence the texture varies a little. The butter-milk and milk left over from making clotted cream were given to the calves and the patient cats.

My family made some cheese but it was not a regular chore as it was on those farms that specialized in Farmhouse cheese.

Skim the cream off the top of the churns especially those that have stood during the night. Place the cream in a large flat metal pan and allow it to stand for 24 hours in winter and 12 in summer. The pan is then placed on a stove, or over a very slow fire and some distance above it, so that it will heat without boiling or even simmering until a solid mass forms on the top. The pan should then be taken to the cool dairy and the cream lifted off when cold. Time—the slower the better.

*Clotted cream keeps much better than raw double cream.*

## BUTTER AND BUTTER MAKING

Butter can be made from milk that has been placed overnight in large shallow basins and in the morning the cream is skimmed off. A more effective method is the use of a machine called a separator. Each day's cream can be added to the same basin and then set aside to ripen or become fit for churning. When the cream is 2 or 3 days old the butter is of a richer colour and flavour. The best temperature at which to churn the cream is about 60°F; if it falls below this, the churning has to continue longer before butter materializes. In hot weather it may be desirable to stand the churn in a basin of cold water to which chips of ice should be added.

The butter churn may be made from wood or be a clear large jar with metal paddles. The churn and paddles must be scalded before use and everything must be thoroughly clean. The top of the churn is taken off and the ripened cream poured in. The churn is then made secure and the handle turned slowly and steadly at first and gradually more quickly, until the revolutions of the paddle are almost sixty a minute. The cream becomes thicker until it is like a thick custard. After a few more turns of the paddle it becomes grainy and little flecks of butter appear. The churn is then opened and a cupful of cold water is thrown in. It is then secured again and the paddle gently turned. After about six turns the grains of butter become bigger, sticking in clots and most of the butter-milk sinks to the bottom. The churn is then opened and its contents poured into a basin and by spoonfuls the butter is lifted out of the buttermilk and placed in the water. The butter is squeezed and kneaded with wooden pats to get rid of the buttermilk. The washing water is changed repeatedly until it remains clear. If buttermilk is left in the butter it will not keep and also has a sour taste. When the last washing water has been drained off, the butter is sprinkled with fine salt and the latter worked in well: this will help to preserve the butter.

The quantity of butter produced from a gallon of milk varies, but it should not fall much below $\frac{1}{2}$ lb. To test salt butter, plunge a knife into it and if when withdrawn the knife has an unpleasant odour, the butter may be regarded as rancid.

# THE MAKING OF CHEESE

In order to make good cheese you will need the following equipment. It is therefore essential that it is available or a substitute can be found before commencing.

1. A table, 6 ft. by 2 ft. with raised sides and ends and lined with tinned sheeting. The table should slope to one corner and have an outlet and pipe to allow the proper drainage of the whey.
2. One or two well made oak tubs in which to coagulate the milk. They should be 6 gallons in capacity with close-fitting wooden lids.
3. A large knife with which to cut the curd.
4. A milk strainer.
5. Curd-ladle.
6. Skimming dish and thermometer.
7. Cheese-draining rack.
8. Set of wall shelves.
9. Measuring glasses.
10. Pails and brushes.
11. Weights up to 28 lbs. with which to press the cheeses.
12. Circular cheese moulds $6\frac{1}{4}$ ins. deep and $6\frac{1}{4}$ ins. in diameter.
13. Length of cheese-grey (cheese cloth).

To make a standard size cheese you require 6 gallons of milk and 2 drams of rennet. Some coarse salt will be needed during the processing.

The milk is first raised to a temperature of 90°F. and the rennet is added to bring about coagulation. The rennet is diluted with six times its volume of water and is then stirred into the milk. The milk is then stirred deeply for 3 to 4 minutes after which the surface is kept gently moving to prevent the fat from rising, until coagulation sets in. The tub or vat is then covered with a wooden lid until coagulation is completed. The curd can be cut approximately 1 hour after the rennet has been added. The curd should be firm and springy and split with a clean fracture when a finger is inserted and lifted upwards through it. Using a long knife the curd is then cut into $\frac{1}{2}$-inch cubes. After cutting the curd is stirred by hand, care being taken to remove particles adhering to the vat. The temperature must now be raised to 106°F. The temperature must not be raised faster than 1° in 3 minutes, and the curd should be stirred during this process. A cheese cloth is then laid over the vat and pressed down on the curd. A supply of whey is then taken off and heated to a temperature of 120°F. and this is returned to the curd. When the curd becomes bright and tough and the particles fall apart when crushed then the whey can be poured off through a straining cloth. The curd is spread evenly over the base of the vat and salt is added to the proportion of 1 oz. to 2 gallons of milk used. The curd is now packed into the moulds which have been previously lined with a cheese cloth and is put to press with 2 cwt. pressure. It is turned the same evening and is in the press until the following morning. In the morning the cheese is taken from the press, sewn in a calico bandage, and again returned to the press for 1 hour, after which it should be placed in a fairly dry draughty room for 2 days and then in a ripening room. It will be ready for use in about 3 weeks when the weight will usually be about $6\frac{1}{2}$ lbs.

# The still room:
# wines and beverages

Christmas just wouldn't be the same without sloe
gin. As long as I can remember we collected
the sloes as soon as they had suffered their first
frost and gathered the other ingredients for sloe
gin. It was a traditional drink at Christmas-time
with other families besides mine. There are many
accounts of land changing hands overnight as folk
played the card game Nap and whiled away the
time sipping sloe gin.

Some of my family were Chapel. They would
also make home-made wines, which were drunk
only for 'medical purposes'.

## SLOE GIN

As soon as the first Autumn frost has been, go and
collect some sloes from the hedgerows. They must
be black in colour. Gather enough sloes to fill a
wide ended bottle or tall jar. Prick each berry well
with a needle and place in the vessel filling it
three-quarters full. Add 4 tablespoonfuls of sugar,
more or less according to your taste, with a tablespoonful of chopped almonds. Fill the jar or
bottle to the neck with neat gin. Give the bottle a
good shake to dissolve the sugar and place in a
dark cool place. Twice a week give the bottle a
good shake. The result is a beautiful plum liquor
that is a heavenly red colour but it is very alcoholic.

*The connoisseurs regulate the end product by the
number of pricks to each berry. They then keep it
for several years. Sloes are the fruit of the blackthorn.*

## DAMSON WINE

*5 lbs. damsons, 4 lbs. sugar, 1 gallon water, 1 lemon,
¾ oz. baker's yeast.*

Remove the stalks, put the damsons into a large
bowl and pour over ½ gallon of boiling water.
Let it cool, then mash with a wooden spoon or
with your hands. Peel the rind of the lemon thinly
and add with the juice. Pour on the other ½ gallon
of water. When luke-warm add the yeast and
sugar, leave for three days. Strain through a
muslin bag. Cover well and leave in a warm place
to finish fermenting. Bottle and place in a cool
place.

## ELDERFLOWER CHAMPAGNE

*You require 7 large heads of elderflowers without
their stalks, 8 pints of cold water, 1½ lbs. sugar, the
rind and juice of 2 lemons, and 2 tablespoonfuls of
wine vinegar.*

Place all the ingredients in a large crock and leave
covered for 4 days. Strain and place in very sound
bottles with good screw tops. It can be drunk after
10 days or if kept, will become a 'still Bordeaux
type' wine.

*The natural yeast in the flowers provides the fizz
and care must be taken as the bottles may explode.*

## DANDELION WINE

Collect the flowers and buds of 4 quarts of dandelions, without the stalks. Pour over the flowers 8 pints of boiling water and 3 lbs. of sugar. Stir well. Add the juice and rind of 2 lemons and 1 orange. When the brew is luke-warm add 1 oz. of yeast. Allow to work for 2 weeks stirring daily. Strain the wine and bottle. Bruised ginger may be added with the lemons.

## LAMB'S WOOL

Heat 1 quart of ale and add 1 pint of cider or white wine, $\frac{1}{2}$ a grated nutmeg, a little cinnamon and some brown sugar. Roast some crab or cider apples and float on top of the liquid in a deep bowl. Serve very hot.

# BEVERAGES

## GINGER BEER

Take 2 lemons and remove the peel very finely. Place the peel in a vessel with the lemon juice, 1 oz. cream of tartar and 3 lbs. of sugar. Boil 1 oz. of crushed root ginger in 2 gallons of water and pour over the other ingredients. Allow the liquid to be luke-warm and then add 2 tablespoonfuls of bakers' yeast. Let it stand for 16 hours and then strain into bottles. Cork them up very tightly. Drink a week later.

# PEPPERMINT CORDIAL

Take 1 lb. of loaf sugar, 1 pint of boiling water and simmer for 10 minutes. Then stir in 1 table-spoonful of honey and when nearly cold add 30 drops of the essence of peppermint. Bottle for use. Essence of ginger can be used in the same way.

# NATURAL LEMONADE

Cut the rind of 3 lemons thinly so as not to have any white on the back. Put in a jug. Strain the juice over 2 or 3 oz. of white sugar. Pour over a quart of hot water and let it stand for 2 hours. Strain and bottle. Lumps of ice broken up and put into this makes a nice summer drink.

# HARVEST DRINK

*4 oz. fine oatmeal, 1 orange, 5 oz. sugar, 1 lemon, 1 gallon of boiling water.*

Put the oatmeal, sugar, juice and the grated rind of the orange and lemon into a pan and mix well with a little warm water. Add the boiling water and stir well. When cold strain and use.

# MAKING A GOOD CUP OF TEA

Be sure to heat the earthen pot,
And have your water boiling hot.
Put in a teaspoonful per cup,
That each of you intend to sup.
Allow to stand for minutes four,
Then off the leaves be sure to pour,
When serving put the milk in first,
Add sugar, and allay your thirst.
With this delightful, fragrant brew
You'll be refreshed and live anew.

*From a very old cookery book.*

# Festive fare

## PLUM PUDDING

¼ lb. stale breadcrumbs, 2 oz. flour, good pinch of salt, ¼ lb. brown sugar, ½ teaspoonful of baking powder, ¼ lb. currants, ¼ lb. Valencia raisins, ¼ lb. sultanas, 2 oz. candied peel (chopped very fine), ¼ teaspoonful grated nutmeg, 1 teaspoonful of mixed spice, grated rind of 1 lemon, ½ oz. ground almonds, ¼ lb. grated suet, 2 large eggs, spirit or milk to mix.

Place into basins and steam for 4 hours.

## SIMNEL CAKE

½ lb. castor sugar, ½ lb. plain flour, 2 teaspoonfuls baking powder, 6 oz. butter, 6 oz. currants, 2 oz. shredded peel, ½ lb. eggs (weighed in their shells). For the almond paste: 6 oz. castor sugar, 3 oz. ground almonds, 1 small egg.

Cream the sugar and butter, add each egg separately and stir in the flour, peel and currants as lightly as possible. Work the ground almonds with the sugar and egg to a stiff paste and roll out to the size of the cake tin. Put half the cake mixture in the tin, then the almond paste and then the remaining mixture. Bake in a moderate oven for 1 hour.

*If you double the amount of almond paste, you can put a layer on top as well and then slide it under the grill to give it a toasted look. You can decorate the top with one small ball to represent each Apostle.*

# CHRISTMAS CAKE

*12 oz. sultanas, 1 lb. flour, 3 teaspoonfuls of baking powder, 6 oz. currants, 12 oz. raisins, ½ teaspoonful of ground ginger, 12 oz. butter, 1 teaspoonful of mixed spice, ½ teaspoonful of ground nutmeg, 12 oz. brown sugar, 1 lemon (juice and rind), 6 eggs, 4 oz. chopped cherries, 2 oz. chopped almonds, 1 oz. candied peel, 2 drops each of vanilla essence and almond essence, 1 glassful of sherry or brandy.*

Line an 8-inch cake tin with greaseproof paper. Cream the butter with the sugar and add the eggs. Beat well, remove the fruit from the sherry/brandy in which it has soaked overnight, and add to the mixture. Keep the liquor. Add all the rest of the ingredients and stir well adding a little liquor if necessary. Cook in a moderate oven for 30 minutes or until the cake has set, then lower the heat to a slow oven and cook for 4 hours. When the cake has been removed from the tin pour the remaining liquor into the base. Cover the whole with almond paste and then cover with royal icing.

# MINCEMEAT

*1 lb. currants, 1 lb. brown sugar, 1 grated nutmeg, ½ teaspoonful of ground cinnamon, ¼ teaspoonful of ground cloves, 1 grated lemon, ½ lb. grated suet, 1 lb. finely chopped apples, juice of 2 lemons, 1 lb. Valencia raisins, ¼ pint of sherry, ¾ glass of rum.*

Mix all together, and keep lightly covered when not in use.

# GOOD FRIDAY DISH

*2 lbs. of salt fish, a dozen oysters or 3 eggs, ¾ pint of milk, 2 heaped tablespoonfuls of flour, 1 teaspoonful of chopped parsley, 1 lb. of potatoes and a little salt.*

Boil the fish that has previously been soaked, when done take up and flake with a fork, put into a large pie dish leaving out the skins and outside pieces. Next make the oyster or egg sauce and pour over the fish. Boil 1 lb. of potatoes with the salt. When done, dry well and put in a potato masher and squeeze over the dish of fish, forming a snow. Sprinkle chopped parsley on top lightly and serve very hot.

*The egg sauce is made from hard-boiled eggs.*

# EASTER BISCUITS

*1 lb. of flour, ½ lb. of butter, 4 oz. castor sugar, 2 oz. of currants, 2 eggs, ½ a wineglass of brandy, and a little mixed spice.*

Cream the butter with the sugar and add the eggs, beat very well. Add the flour and spice and mix in well. Add the brandy and currants and stir in. Roll out thinly and bake in a moderate oven for 10 minutes. Sprinkle castor sugar on top as they leave the oven.

*Watch the cooking of these biscuits closely as they should be pale in colour and will burn very quickly. My grandmother was given this recipe by a baker living on the Somerset levels and it was sought by many interested cooks. It does not use oil of cassia which is traditional in most Easter biscuits.*

# HOT CROSS BUNS

In 1¼ pints of milk melt 2 oz. butter or lard. Allow it to be luke-warm and then add to 1 oz of compressed yeast and 1 teaspoonful of sugar. Stir well until the yeast has dissolved. Drop in a lightly beaten egg. Pour this liquid into 2 lbs. of strong flour that has ½ teaspoonful of mixed spice added. Put in a warm place to double in size. Knead it well and incorporate 4 oz. of currants. Make into bun shapes and place on a greased baking tray. Allow to rise again and cook in a hot oven for 10 minutes. Remove and mark with a cross made from water and flour mixed. Return to the hot oven and cook for another 5 minutes. Glaze the buns with a milk and sugar mixture and allow to dry slightly in the oven.

*Again oil of cassia is usually used in Hot Cross buns. Some households had a wooden press that had a cross carved out of it and they pressed on each bun to shape the cross.*

# HARVEST CAKE

Mix together 6 oz. dripping or lard and 6 oz. brown sugar, add 1½ lbs. of flour, 3 teaspoonfuls of baking powder, 6 oz. currants and a teaspoonful of mixed spice. Mix well with an egg and a little milk if necessary. Bake in a shallow tin and sprinkle the top with brown sugar.

*In the middle of Granny's cook book was this list that must have been written there for safe keeping. It speaks for itself.*

## HARVEST SUPPER LIST

Tables.
Forms.
Table clothes.
6 lamps.
$3\frac{1}{2}$ dozen dinner plates.
$3\frac{1}{2}$ dozen pudding plates.
$3\frac{1}{2}$ dozen tumblers.
2 jugs.
$3\frac{1}{2}$ dozen knives.
$3\frac{1}{2}$ dozen forks.
16 table spoons.
2 gravy spoons.
2 carving knives and forks.
8 salts.
8 salt spoons.
8 mustard pots.
8 mustard spoons.
6 pepper pots.
16 vegetable dishes.

# Index

[95]